LEARNIN
ONLY MI

MW00655419

LESS STRESS IN 30 DAYS is a stress management program with daily exercises that take only 15 to 20 minutes to complete and can be easily integrated into your life. Checklists and charts help you identify the common causes of stress and how it can affect you in ways such as headaches, loss of memory, nightmares, and overeating. You will learn to become familiar with the things that push *your* stress buttons and how to work through your tension. With muscle relaxation, breathing, and visualization techniques, this integrated program can bring increased vitality, improved mental and physical health, and inner satisfaction. The benefits are concrete, immediate, and long lasting.

"An excellent and extremely practical guide for teaching yourself how to relax, and how to respond with greater balance and effectiveness in stressful situations."

—Jon Kabat-Zinn, Ph.D.,
Director of the Stress Reduction and Relaxation Clinics, University of Massachusetts Medical School

PEGGY ROGGENBUCK GILLESPIE was Assistant Director and is a Consultant to the Stress Reduction Department at the University of Massachusetts Medical Center. She also has a private practice at the Belchertown Wellness Center.

LYNN BECHTEL coordinates educational workshops and groups at the Mental Health division of the University of Massachusetts Health Services.

LESS STRESS IN 30 DAYS

An Integrated Program for Relaxation

Peggy Roggenbuck Gillespie,
M.L.S., C.S.W.

and

Lynn Bechtel,
M.ED., L.C.S.W.

*With a Foreword by
Daniel Goleman, Ph.D.*

A SIGNET BOOK

NEW AMERICAN LIBRARY

NAL BOOKS ARE AVAILABLE AT QUANTITY DISCOUNTS WHEN USED TO PROMOTE PRODUCTS OR SERVICES. FOR INFORMATION PLEASE WRITE TO PREMIUM MARKETING DIVISION, NEW AMERICAN LIBRARY, 1633 BROADWAY, NEW YORK, NEW YORK 10019

PUBLISHER'S NOTE

The ideas, procedures, and suggestions contained in this book are not intended as a substitute for consulting with your physician. All matters regarding your health require medical supervision.

Grateful acknowledgment is made to the following for permission to reprint excerpts from:

The Stress of Life by Hans Selye. Copyright © 1978 by Hans Selye. Reprinted by permission of McGraw-Hill.

Love by Leo Buscaglia. Copyright © 1972 by Leo F. Buscaglia. Reprinted by permission of the author.

Be Young and Flexible After 30, 40, 50, 60 . . . by Ruth Bender. Copyright © 1976 by Ruth Bender. Reprinted by permission of Ruben Publishers.

A Course in Miracles by the Foundation for Inner Peace, Inc. Copyright © 1975. Reprinted by permission of the Foundation for Inner Peace.

(The following page constitutes an extension of the copyright page.)

This book previously appeared in a Plume edition.

SIGNET, SIGNET CLASSIC, MENTOR, ONYX, PLUME, MERIDIAN and NAL BOOKS are published by NAL PENGUIN INC., 1633 Broadway, New York, New York 10019

First Signet Edition, August, 1987

4 5 6 7 8 9

PRINTED IN THE UNITED STATES OF AMERICA

This book is dedicated to all the clients and workshop participants we have worked with at University of Massachusetts Medical Center, the Belchertown Wellness Center, the Cancer Counseling and Research Center, the Tulsa Psychiatric Center, Interface, Medical West, and the University of Massachusetts Health Services for serving as our inspiration and teaching us so much over the years. It has been a privilege working with all of you.

Contents

Acknowledgments

LESS STRESS IN 30 DAYS brings together a synthesis of the work of many experts in the fields of psychology, stress, and meditation. It would take too long to thank them all for their contributions but every author listed in our Suggested Readings has been a great help in our work. Specifically, we want to mention the pioneering work and research done by Dr. Jon Kabat-Zinn, Director of the Stress Reduction and Relaxation Program at University of Massachusetts Medical Center, Worcester, Massachusetts. In his dedication to the work of helping people understand and reduce their stress reactions, he has developed an innovative approach which has inspired many programs throughout the country.

Also, we would like to acknowledge Mark Sokol, formerly of the Special Consultation and Treatment Program for Women, Worcester, Massachusetts; and Pam Gonyer, Health Educator at University Health Services, University of Massachusetts, Amherst, Massachusetts, for their knowledge, ideas about stress management education, and collegial support.

We want to thank some people who helped by reading and commenting on the manuscript in its early stages: Virginia Ackerman, whose support and many specific comments were invaluable; Deborah Robson, who typed, copyedited, and made useful changes; Rita Tinsley and Mary Hastings, who critiqued the book and gave encouragement; Vicki Van Steenberg, who gave helpful comments and encouragement; Martine Lund, who made many significant copyediting changes; Karen Thatcher, for her speedy and accurate typing; and finally, Tara Bennett-Goleman and Dan Goleman for their strong encouragement, their editorial suggestions, their belief in this book, and their help in getting it into the public eye.

At NAL, we want to thank Mitch Rose for his excellent work as editor. In his friendly, warm way he helped us feel confident and his suggestions were always right on the mark. The copy editor, Bruce Magenheimer, did a superb job with stylistic changes and helped make the book more readable. In fact, he did all of the Less Stress lessons himself, to make sure the directions were clear.

And finally, our literary agent, Susan Ann Protter, deserves many thanks for her help. We appreciate her energy and enthusiasm.

On a personal note, Lynn would like to thank her sister, Barbara Hornby, for inspiration by example; and Peggy would like to thank her husband, Gregory Gillespie, for his constant support of this project.

Foreword

Stress is an inevitable part of living—to be alive is to change. And our *reaction* to change is the essence of stress.

Since we can't avoid stress, it behooves us to learn to deal with it. If we don't, it will do us in. If we deal with it effectively, our physical and mental health will be enriched.

Consider the hundreds of studies that show a relationship between life changes, such as a divorce or a career move, and disease. The research demonstrates that, for most of us, going through periods where we undergo many such changes in a short time is likely to lead to our becoming ill —sometimes seriously ill—within several months following the changes.

But though the relationship between life changes and illness has been shown valid in studies of thousands of people, the link is not binding. In those same studies there are many thousands of people who go through many, many intense changes, and emerge none the worse for it. Indeed, there are some who thrive on change.

Researchers have identified a set of personality traits that they call "hardiness." Hardy people, they find, simply do not fall prey to illness when their lives get stressful. In fact, the hardy love change, and lots of it.

One of the key traits of these people is that they do not see changes as stressful—they see them as challenges. And therein lies one key to handling stress. Hans Selye, the physician who first described the stress syndrome, has distinguished between stress which leads to disease, and "eustress," the kind of challenge that people find invigorating. Eustress, said Selye, is what makes life interesting, even exciting.

But exactly which life events you find stressful, and which you think are exciting challenges depends much less on the events themselves than on how you see them. Take, for example, getting a new job, or moving to a new city. If you just worry about the things that could go wrong at the new job, or think only about how lonely you will be in that new city, then these changes will be stressful. But if you look forward to the new opportunities the job offers you, or to the new people you will meet when you move to another city, then those changes are simply challenges to be met, new possibilities to be seized.

In order to turn stress into eustress, it helps to tackle multiple fronts, both physical and mental—for stress affects you both ways. Stress is not just the body's reactions—a heightened blood pressure and racing pulse—nor is it just the mind's worries and ruminations. It is both.

That is where the Less Stress Program comes in. Peggy Roggenbuck Gillespie and Lynn Bechtel are highly experienced stress counselors, and they have drawn on the very best techniques in the field to develop their program for helping you ease stress. The result is a superb set of stress-fighting tools. Their program offers antidotes to stress that work on all physical and mental fronts and that you can use at your own pace in the way that best suits your individual needs.

In research I conducted while at Harvard, I found that people who had the habit of devoting a few minutes each day to a stress-fighting technique were healthier, more relaxed, and more alert than people who simply let themselves be buffeted by stress. Over the last two decades, researchers and clinicians have developed dozens and dozens of techniques that can serve as a daily stress antidote.

In developing the Less Stress Program, Peggy Roggenbuck Gillespie and Lynn Bechtel have selected the most effective, and arranged them in a uniquely useful combination. If you would like to make your life more relaxed and richer, and make yourself more full of energy and joy, I recommend the Less Stress program to you most highly.

—Daniel Goleman, Ph.D., *The New York Times*

Introduction

Most people today are aware of the toll chronic stress can take on their lives. Everyone wants to feel healthier, happier, and more relaxed, yet many of us lead such busy, active lives that finding the time to take a stress-management class or to read a long, complicated book about stress may seem like an impossible task.

As professionals in the field of stress management, we have worked with thousands of men and women, of all ages and educational levels, who wanted to learn to manage their daily stress. And we know that for each person who comes to seek our help, there are hundreds who don't have the time, money, or access to stress-management classes. So we decided to write a very concise, easy-to-use, day-by-day guide to stress-management skills. *Less Stress in 30 Days* won't teach you much about the physiology of stress—we have included a list of references at the back of the book for anyone who wants to study this topic in more depth—but *we will teach you how to be more relaxed.*

We all have times when we wonder if we can survive the difficulties in our life. At such times everything we do seems permeated with tension, worry, and anxiety. Sometimes life, itself, seems impossible to survive—it presents us with constant and unpredictable changes. So, how can we learn to live with dignity, balance, humor, relaxation, and inner peace? How can we survive life's daily frustrations and losses?

The Chinese say that in every crisis there is an opportunity. We agree. Every situation, no matter how painful, offers us the chance to grow and to develop insight and compassion. In the Less Stress Program we want to give you some tools to help you go beyond mere survival and into a life of more joy. We want you to know that it is possible to change unhealthy habits, behaviors, and attitudes once you have made the decision and the commitment to participate in improving your own mind and body. It *is* possible to develop an increased ability to relax, greater enthusiasm for life, self-esteem, and better ways of responding to stressful situations. The Less Stress Lessons can motivate you to help yourself as you learn to introduce practical, productive, and positive changes into your life on a daily basis.

In our own lives we have found that our creative output, our enjoyment of relationships, and our energy levels have increased by practicing the Less Stress Lessons. But this hasn't come easily. As much as we all would like the stress and suffering in our lives to disappear magically, we know that learning to relax involves some difficult, but deeply rewarding work. We still have to stay alert in order to recognize our habitual stress reaction patterns, and we certainly have not eliminated all of our anxieties and fears. We realize that learning to manage stress is going to be a lifetime proposition, but if you follow our program, you will have the same tools we've used successfully with our clients and ourselves.

Learning to relax will take only *minutes* of your day. When you discover the benefits of the Less Stress Lessons, you'll find that you can be relaxed even in the midst of a "crazy" day.

We know the Less Stress Lessons can work for you if you will work with them regularly. These Lessons are only the beginning of a road that can lead you toward increased vitality, improved mental and physical health, and inner peace. Where else is there to go?

—Peggy Roggenbuck Gillespie and Lynn Bechtel

Before You Begin: A Warning

If you are chronically depressed, suffer from frequent anxiety attacks, or have phobias or severe health problems—including alcoholism, drug dependencies, or eating disorders that interfere with your ability to function normally—we strongly urge you to seek outside help. In these circumstances please follow the Less Stress Program only under the support and guidance of a qualified therapist. If you have physical symptoms you believe are stress-related, we also urge you to have a thorough checkup by a physician before beginning the Less Stress Program.

If you have recently gone through a major life change—the death of a loved one, divorce, marriage, the birth of a child, change of jobs, loss of a job—you might find it very helpful to be in therapy along with following the Less Stress Program. You also can find or start your own support group in your community. The love and support of people who know what you're going through can be very therapeutic.

Even if your stress-related problems are not severe, we believe that good therapy—individual, family, or group—can greatly enhance the work you will be doing in the Less Stress Lessons. Remember, it is not necessary to wait until you are desperate to seek help. Asking for help is a sign of inner strength and of a strong motivation to make changes, not, as some people mistakenly believe, a sign of weakness or giving up.

Nadine Stair wrote this poem when she was eighty-five years old:

If I Had My Life to Live Over

I'd like to make more mistakes next time.
I'd relax. I would limber up. I would be sillier
than I have been this trip. I would take fewer
things seriously. I would take more chances. I
would climb more mountains and swim more
rivers. I would eat more ice cream and less beans.
I would perhaps have more actual troubles, but
I'd have fewer imaginary ones.

You see, I'm one of those people who live sensibly
and sanely hour after hour, day after day. Oh,
I've had my moments, and if I had it to do over
again, I'd have more of them. In fact, I'd try to
have nothing else. Just moments, one after
another, instead of living so many years ahead
of each day. I've been one of those persons who
never goes anywhere without a thermometer, a
hot water bottle, a raincoat, and a parachute.
If I had to do it again, I would travel lighter
than I have.

If I had my life to live over, I would start
barefoot earlier in the spring and stay that way
later in the fall. I would go to more dances. I
would ride more merry-go-rounds. I would pick
more daisies.

—Nadine Stair

WHY WAIT UNTIL YOU ARE EIGHTY-FIVE TO BEGIN LIVING EACH MOMENT MORE FULLY?

PART I

What Is Stress?
What Is Relaxation?

What Is Stress?

Stress, in itself, is neither good nor bad. You need a little stress to give your life some zing, to help you do your best. Stress is simply the way your body responds to any change in life or any challenge whether it is big, small, good, or bad. If you go from a warm room into the cold air, get a raise, get fired, run two blocks to catch a bus, get married, or get divorced, you experience some effects of stress.

The physical changes indicating that you are under stress —tight shoulders, clammy hands, headache, upset stomach, tight chest, etc.—result from the arousal of many bodily systems. This state of arousal is frequently called the *fight-or-flight response*. This is a completely natural and instinctive response of the body to a life-threatening situation.

Marsha J., 29, single, insurance executive

Marsha came home from work late one night. She lives alone in the second-floor apartment of a two-family house, and her downstairs neighbors were away on vacation. Everything seemed okay when Marsha first came into the house, but when she came upstairs toward her apartment door, she heard a noise—possibly a footstep. She thought the noise was probably just her cat jumping off the bookcase. But she held her briefcase more tightly and became more aware of her surroundings. Marsha's hand was shaky when she unlocked the door, and she knew almost immediately after stepping inside the front hall that something was wrong. When she turned on the light, she saw that someone had been in the apartment; the contents of the hall closet were strewn all over the floor, and in the living room her books were torn out of the bookcase and the desk drawers pulled out and emptied. She heard the sound of footsteps coming toward her from the back of the apartment. She shouted and ran, faster than she'd ever run before, downstairs and across the street to a neighbor's house.

Marsha chose flight; some people might choose to confront the intruder. In either case the body goes through significant changes.

Whenever the brain perceives an event as threatening—the threat can be actual, as Marsha's intruder was; or emotional, like a verbal attack by the boss; or even imaginary, like worrying about the possible outcome of an upcoming event—the physiological response is basically the same. Here's what happens:

STRESSOR (Threat)
|
perceived by
|
BRAIN
|
which activates
|
ADRENAL GLANDS
|
which release
adrenaline-related hormones
into
|
BLOODSTREAM

Some of the internal changes that occur during the fight-or-flight response are:

- Increased heart rate
- Elevated blood pressure

- Increased breathing rate; breathing becomes rapid and shallow
- Release of stored energy from the liver into the bloodstream
- Dilation of pupils to let in more light
- Heightening of all senses
- Tensing of muscles for movement or protective actions
- Activation of blood-clotting mechanisms
- Shutdown of digestive processes; blood diverted to muscles and the brain
- Constriction of blood flow to the extremities
- Sweating.

Once the immediate threat is gone, you let go. You feel weak and tired as the stress hormones begin to recede, and your body eventually returns to its normal state of equilibrium.

How Stress Becomes Distress

In the 1930s Dr. Hans Selye began to do research showing the results of sustained physiological arousal on living organisms. In 1956 Dr. Selye published his landmark work, *The Stress of Life*, in which he defined stress as "the rate of wear and tear in the body" and the stressor as the stressful event that activated the automatic arousal system. Selye called the entire process of stress reactivity the General Adaptation Syndrome (GAS), which he divided into four phases:

1. *Alarm:* This is the fight-or-flight response.
2. *Resistance:* This is the stage in which the body attempts

to adapt to the physiological changes occurring from the alarm state.

3. *Exhaustion:* If the arousal continues, the body's attempt to create a balance, in addition to the physiological effects of the alarm arousal, leads to a depletion of reserve fuel and to a state of exhaustion. Symptoms begin to appear.
4. *Termination:* If there is no relief from the arousal, the stress on the physiological system can lead to death.[1]

Selye's conclusions indicate that when the source of stress is prolonged or undefined, or when several sources exist at once, an individual may not return to a normal mental and physiological baseline. He or she will continue to manifest potentially damaging stress reactions, which often show up in symptoms or early warning signs of excessive strain on the mind/body system. June's story provides a good example.

June M., 36, single, administrative assistant

June is an administrative assistant to the director of a social service agency that works with troubled adolescents. June left for the office on a Friday knowing she might have a bad day. She has been frustrated and resentful about some of the more routine things she has to do; she'd like the opportunity to take on more responsibility. Her work had been piling up all week, and one of the secretaries was ill, so June was stuck doing extra work. To make things worse, she'd been having trouble concentrating.

The day certainly lived up to June's expectations. Her boss gave June two long reports to edit and type, then kept changing them when June was halfway through, so that she had to start all over again. She was angry but didn't feel she could do

[1] Hans Selye, *The Stress of Life* (New York: McGraw Hill, 1956), pp. 79–83.

anything about it. She couldn't punch her boss or run out of the office forever. Her resentment smoldered, and her body never got a chance to return to a normal balance.

By the end of the day June had a headache that felt like something was squeezing her scalp, and she had pain in her neck and shoulders. Rush-hour traffic didn't help June's mood. She almost had an accident when someone stopped suddenly in front of her, and her fight-or-flight response was triggered again. June could feel her shoulders knotting up as she drove, and when she finally got home, she felt miserable. June's body remained in a chronic state of stress-preparedness.

Stress Cues

Now that you've seen how stress has affected June, it's time to look at your own symptoms of distress. Identifying these symptoms is an important step toward managing stress. But remember, stress is only one of the possible causes of these symptoms. There could be other physical causes for any of them. Be sure to check with your physician if symptoms persist or interfere with daily functioning. This book cannot take the place of professional treatment.

Stress Checklist

Physical Symptoms

Headaches	______
Digestive problems	______
Insomnia	______
Oversleeping	______
Rashes or other skin problems	______
Sexual difficulties	______
Elevated blood pressure	______
Chest pain	______
Heart palpitations	______
Loss of appetite	______
Always hungry	______
Neck or back spasms	______
Chronic fatigue	______
Jaw pain	______
Dizzy spells	______
Nausea	______
Frequent urination	______
Nail-biting	______
Body warmer or colder than usual	______
Night sweats	______
Constant perspiration	______

Emotional Symptoms

Increased moodiness	______
Withdrawal from other people	______
Difficulty concentrating	______
Loss of memory	______
Increased restlessness	______
Frenetic activity	______
Difficulty making decisions	______
Annoyed by little things	______
Shy or overly sensitive	______
Frequent crying	______
Considered suicide	______
Fear of criticism	______
Angered easily	______
Nightmares	______
Hopeless outlook	______

Behavioral Symptoms

Finger-tapping	______
Foot-tapping	______
Compulsive eating	______
Nail-biting	______
Hair-pulling	______
Repetitive thoughts	______

Increased smoking	______
Increased alcohol use	______
Increased drug use	______
Work absenteeism or lateness	______
Decreased productivity	______
Nonstop talking	______

After you finish the Less Stress Lessons, return to this checklist and see if you have eliminated any symptoms.

Diseases of Adaptation

For humans, especially in the comparative safety of the Western world, the major source of stress is not the external environment, but the emotional and perceptual factors that dictate an individual's response to other people, life events, and stressful situations. Consider Joe B.'s case.

Joe B., 39, married, psychotherapist

Joe works in a clinic where he sees clients in short-term treatment and also has some administrative responsibility. He strives toward perfection and considers himself a failure when he achieves anything less, which is all the time.

As a child, Joe always dreaded bringing report cards home because his father demanded *A*'s. Nothing less was acceptable. Perfection was the norm in his house. So now, at age 39, Joe has ended up with an ulcer. As his anxiety and impatience with his physical condition increase, his attacks of pain become more severe, and his anxiety increases yet again. Preoccupied with ill health, he feels less competent at work. Joe is caught up in a vicious cycle.

Dr. Selye showed that when arousal is maintained over an extended period of time, serious damage to the vital organs can result. When this chronic reactivity results in illness, the anxiety associated with the illness itself may feed into the continuing cycle of stress.

Dr. Selye conclusively proved in animal research that ordinary diseases can develop as a result of unabated General Adaptation Syndrome (GAS), with such factors as heredity, environment, general health habits, and past illnesses as the variables that determine whether illness will occur and what part of the body will be affected. Selye states:

> When it fails to cope adequately with a potential disease-producing situation, the body develops what I have called stress diseases or diseases of adaptation . . . which factor in: high blood pressure, diseases of the heart, diseases of the kidney, inflammatory diseases of the skin and eyes, infections, allergic diseases, nervous and mental diseases, digestive disorders, any metabolic diseases, cancer and diseases of resistance in general.[2]

Although Selye and researchers before him used animals in their studies, humans seem to have an even greater capacity to react to subtle levels of stress, because of their intellectual and emotional sensitivity.

---

[2] Hans Selye, *Stress Without Distress* (New York: Signet, 1976), pp. 169–70.

Medical Treatment of Stress-Related Disorders

Until recently, medical intervention for the treatment of stress-related disorders has relied almost exclusively on medications for symptom control. For the common disorders diagnosed as muscular or nervous tension, 144 million new prescriptions, many for drugs with unpleasant side effects, were written in just one year. According to a June 6, 1983, *Time* magazine cover story on stress, "It is a sorry sign of the times that the three bestselling drugs in the country are an ulcer medication (Tagamet), a hypertension drug (Inderal), and a muscle relaxant (Valium)." Fortunately, in the past twenty years, there has been a growing interest in nonpharmacologic methods to prevent and heal diseases which have been demonstrated to have emotional components.

In the 1950s and 1960s many people became dissatisfied with the highly technological aspects of Western life and migrated philosophically, if not literally, to Asian cultures. Among these travelers were physicians, psychologists, scientists, and lay people who discovered that ancient medical techniques differed radically from modern Western methods. They were exposed to mysteries such as acupuncture, which emphasized prevention of disease by balancing physical, emotional, and spiritual energies. They also observed meditators (yogis), who had learned to consciously control bodily functions, such as heart rate and blood pressure, which previously were considered by Western science to be beyond human voluntary control. Medications made from natural substances were prescribed only after an individual's psychosocial and spiritual life were taken into account. A common factor seen in all of these Asian medical traditions was the emphasis on the treatment of the whole person—mind, body, *and* spirit—as a key to health.

Research in the United States and Europe on these ancient methods has led to the creation of a new medical model combining the best of Western and Asian medical knowledge. New departments of pain control, behavioral, and preventive medicine have begun to sprout within many traditional hospitals, almost all incorporating some non-drug, self-regulatory methods for the treatment of stress-related diseases. According to Ken Pelletier, M.D., author of *Mind as Healer/Mind as Slayer:*

> It is increasingly unlikely that a pharmacological panacea will resolve the fundamental issue of illness and health. . . . If an individual can learn how to respond to a stressful stimuli to which a Fight-or-Flight response would be inappropriate, by inducing a state of relaxed, non-aroused physiological function, he or she will be able to avoid the consequences of a prolonged stress reaction.[3]

What Is Relaxation?

Many people believe that relaxation is the exact opposite of tension. They picture themselves lying around the house or office, as useless as a limp strand of linguine, unable to move, think, or act decisively. Two people we met were actually terrified of relaxation.

Jack H., 35, a building contractor, said, "Sure, I want to get rid of my colitis, but I also need to appear strong and

[3] Kenneth Pelletier, *Mind as Healer, Mind as Slayer* (New York: Delacorte, 1977), pp. 35–36.

confident, especially at work. I certainly don't want to become known as a space cadet, or else some cross-legged, do-nothing yogi mumbling weird chants under my breath."

Ellen G., 31, is a nurse and the single parent of a four-year-old boy. She asked, "What if I become too relaxed and turn into a zombie? I wouldn't be able to give good care to my patients, I'd screw up in emergencies, I'd be too tired to take care of my child, and men would find me utterly boring. You know, like Catherine. She seems so calm; she barely says a word to anyone or lifts a finger at work. I'd rather be my regular, frazzled self than be that relaxed. At least everyone thinks of me as a live wire."

Unfortunately for them, Ellen and Jack have no idea what relaxation really is. In fact, Ellen is calling Catherine's behavior relaxed when actually Catherine might be shy, tired, or depressed. Jack assumes that being relaxed requires a complete change of personality. Their misconceptions and fears prevent them from learning some very basic ways of being in the world in a relaxed *and* energetic manner.

In order to understand relaxation on a physical level, try the following exercise.

Posture Scan

1. Stand in front of a full-length mirror and close your eyes.
   Mentally scan your body from your toes all the way up to the top of your head, noting:
   - Areas of tension, tightness, constriction
   - Areas that feel relaxed, loose, comfortable
   - Areas that feel numb or lack any sensation.
2. Notice how you are standing (you can open your eyes if you need to):
   - Knees locked, or bent in a relaxed way?
   - Stomach held tight or released?
   - Shoulders forward or back?

- One side of your body more tense than the other?
- Weight distributed evenly?
- Head forward, or balanced on top of spine?

3. Now begin to *exaggerate* the areas of tension. Don't be afraid to look or feel silly. If your shoulders are hunched forward a bit, push them as far forward as you can without straining. If your lower back is swayed back, then exaggerate the sway.

   Hold this posture and open your eyes. Notice how you look. Walk around. Notice how you feel. Hold the exaggerated posture for a few seconds more.

   Now release the extra tension. Notice how you feel as you let go.
4. Close your eyes and scan your body again.
   - Has your posture changed?
   - Are you more aware of tense areas in your body?
   - Do you feel more relaxed now?

Even though you exaggerated your normal level of tension, the posture scan exercise demonstrates how tension can use up a great deal of your physical energy. The chronic tension you carry around in your body every day can be partially responsible for all sorts of problems. When you put so much of your energy into keeping your body tense, you look and feel years older than you really are. It's exhausting to be tense!

Relaxation = Energy

With a relaxed body and mind you can conserve all that added energy for enjoying life. As you follow the Less Stress Lessons, you will learn to balance your periods of activity with special times for relaxation breaks, and to examine your reactions to stressful situations throughout the day. Becoming relaxed can allow you to be more sensual and sexier, as well as more organized and efficient. The more relaxed and aware you become, the more you will be able to revitalize your body and mind, and increase your productivity and your enthusiasm for life. When you are more relaxed, you won't always react automatically to situations in your old, habitual way. A relaxed person has more choices and, therefore, much more freedom.

Relaxation is the best gift you can give yourself!

Different Levels of Relaxation

There are many levels of relaxation, ranging from the absence of noticeable tension in the mind and body to the experience of deep inner states of psychological or spiritual peace. For the purpose of this book we would like to define two basic levels of relaxation.

1. *Physiological relaxation.* This type of relaxation is characterized by changes in the body that are opposite in almost all respects to the fight-or-flight response. Some of the major changes that occur are the slowing down of breath and heart rates, a decrease in oxygen consumption, and the lowering or stabilization of blood pressure. Physiological relaxation can be taught with the use of a variety of well-researched techniques, such as biofeedback, many forms of meditation such as Dr. Benson's Relaxation Response, Dr. Jacobsen's Progressive Relaxation, and diaphragmatic breathing.

2. *Deep inner relaxation.* This type of relaxation is char-

acterized by changes in one's mind state. According to Dr. Jon Kabat-Zinn, director of the Stress Reduction Department at the University of Massachusetts Medical Center:

> The deepest relaxation is a sense of being at home in your own skin and being comfortable with who you are. By learning to direct your energy into a more aware observation of your changes in circumstances and mood, you will be developing this deeper level of relaxation. The *awareness itself* is the essential ingredient for maximum clinical improvement in our patients, rather than any of the specific combination of relaxation techniques a patient chooses to use.

In the Less Stress Lessons you will learn ways to achieve both physiological and deep inner relaxation.

How Do You Relax?

There are as many ways to relax as there are people, and there is no one right way to relax. When we asked a large group of people to tell us their favorite ways of relaxing, here is a partial list of what they said:

- Curling up with a great book, especially a whodunit
- Taking a walk alone, preferably in natural surroundings
- Watching television
- Reading the newspaper from cover to cover
- Having some wine or beer
- Taking a nap
- Taking a long soak in the tub with the bathroom door locked
- Organizing and restoring my collection of antique clocks

- Watching a sports event (on TV or in person)
- Backpacking in the mountains in summer, skiing in winter
- The first puff on a cigarette
- A gourmet meal followed by a rich chocolate dessert
- Sailing my Sunfish
- A long phone conversation with my closest friend
- Playing video games on my personal computer
- Baking bread.
- Whatever exercise I'm into these days. Now it's weight lifting.
- Having great sex
- Playing a fast game of racquetball
- Shopping for new clothes.

What would you add to this list?

My favorite ways to relax are:	How often do I use this method?
1. ____________________	1. ____________________
2. ____________________	2. ____________________
3. ____________________	3. ____________________
4. ____________________	4. ____________________
5. ____________________	5. ____________________

Many of these commonly used methods of relaxation, such as exercising, taking a walk, sexual intercourse, a long bath, hobbies, etc., are very healthy choices. Indeed, they can bring you a deep sense of pleasure and release from daily tension. If you are already doing such activities on a regular basis, keep going. The Less Stress Lessons will complement what you are already doing. But remember: with all these activities you can still be functioning at a high level of mental or physical tension, depending on your inner attitude and approach. You can worry about your problems even while making love, taking a bath, or exercising.

Roy F., 47, divorced, commercial photographer

Roy began a jogging program six months ago as part of his medical treatment for the heart attack he had last year. He used to be very athletic during high school and college—he had been an all-star basketball player—but over the years he had given up exercising because of the increasing demands of his job. Now he runs after work with a coed running club, and many of its members are younger and in much better shape than Roy. He has been pushing himself harder and harder, trying to run faster and farther every day. Instead of feeling more relaxed after jogging, Roy feels tense and frustrated. His feelings of competition interfere with his ability to use his exercise time for relaxation.

Other items on the relaxation list, such as watching TV and reading, will certainly allow you to unwind after a long day at the office or at home with your kids. However, many books, and certainly the daily newspaper and the television, bombard you with a great deal of stressful information. Reading about—or watching—the latest plane crash, hostage situation, or leak of toxic wastes into nearby water supplies may seem just part of an ordinary evening at home. But don't fool yourself. These activities may be interesting, but they will not create deep physiological relaxation.

To see this more clearly, try scanning your body for tension while you are watching the evening news, your favorite police drama, or the final moments of an exciting sports event. We're not suggesting that watching television or reading are bad for your health, but we are asking you to be realistic when you calculate the amount of actual physiological relaxation time you allow yourself to have every day.

And don't overlook the fact that some of the ways people "relax" are actually major contributors to their stress and health problems. *Overconsumption* of alcohol, caffeine, sugar, cigarettes, or drugs is definitely not the solution to stress. Although these addictions may fool you into feeling momentarily relaxed, your reliance on such methods will ultimately undermine your quest for improved physical and emotional health.

A Special Time to Relax?

As you can see from the list of common relaxation methods, almost all of these methods require special times of the day. Most of them involve some kind of activity. But what if you are feeling tense because you are late for an important job interview? The traffic is horrible, and you feel your stomach knotting up. Obviously, if you are driving, you can't take out a novel and start reading, nor can you easily get out of the car and begin to do your aerobic routine on the highway. If your boss is very critical and you feel like punching him, you can't turn on the television and watch a football game to get rid of your aggression. You might be able to do your exercises if you are lucky enough to have your own office, but chances are that your schedule of free time and your boss's outburst won't coincide. And, after a long day, a bath can be a delightful place to relax—as long as you get into the bathroom before your roommates, kids, or spouse have used up all the hot water.

Real-Life Relaxation

It is essential to find methods of relaxation that not only teach you to achieve physiological states of relaxation during practice periods, but also become part of your entire life—methods that can travel with you everywhere you go throughout your craziest day. And you need to know enough methods so that you have several options for different situations.

Caroline R., 23, single, actress

Caroline is finally facing those "cattle calls" she heard so much about in acting school—the judging faces and the probable rejections. She says, "I need to glow with energy and relaxation while I'm on the line being stared at, as well as during the actual audition. I've tried meditation and it works fine when I have time to do it, but the effect only lasts for about an hour. If I tried to meditate in the middle of a job interview, they'd think I was nuts. And that certainly won't help me to pay the rent.

Caroline definitely needs to find other ways to relax—ways that will help her to cope with a variety of stressful experiences.

Awareness Is the Key

At the core of the Less Stress Lessons is our strong belief that you can learn to live your life more harmoniously, with more continuous periods of physiological and deep inner relaxation. This doesn't mean that you will never feel anxious, worried, or tense; these are normal states of mind that are appropriate in certain situations. But it does mean that you can learn to balance the amount and degree of tension in your life.

By closely observing your body, you will begin to see how patterns of physical tension may be creating unnecessary pain and other unpleasant symptoms. By closely observing your mind, you will begin to see how certain emotional patterns—of fear, worrying, reactivity, craving, holding on to negative self-images or anger, refusing to accept the impermanence of life itself—create suffering in the mind. Once you are able to see that your reactions to many of the stressful events in your life are habitual, conditioned patterns of behavior, you can begin to move from the stance of being a "victim of circumstances" to a more powerful and hopeful position where change is possible.

Insight into your behavior can create the strong inner motivation necessary for you to be successful in the self-directed Less Stress Program.

This Is Not a Band-Aid Approach

In our work in hospitals, clinics, and with university students, we've used and studied many of the most popular techniques of relaxation training. In the Less Stress Lessons we have synthesized what we consider the best of all the major methods available. You will start by learning some excellent techniques of physiological relaxation; however, real-life stress management will involve more than learning techniques. You must be willing to go deeper. This will involve the exploration of your attitudes and feelings, and the willingness to work on discovering and practicing new ways of seeing and responding to the inevitable stresses in daily life. Almost every Less Stress Lesson will offer you something you can actually use throughout the day.

Practicing Awareness

As you follow the Less Stress Lessons, the special practice periods we recommend you do each day will help you to become familiar with techniques and concepts that you will be able to adapt to fit your own unique life-style. Awareness can be practiced everywhere, in every situation: while walking, sitting, lying down, eating, exercising, working, talking, or making love. As you bring awareness into every aspect of your mind and body, you can move away from the automatic pilot way of living and into a more spontaneous, joyful appreciation of life as it unfolds.

Larry E., 41, married, father of two children, surgeon

Larry recently recovered from a triple bypass operation, and he said, "I was sick and tired of living my life without really experiencing most of it. I'd jump out of bed every morning at five forty-five sharp, run to the bathroom, brush my teeth, bolt my breakfast while reading the news, drive as fast as I could to the hospital, work all day without having one nonmedical conversation, drink at least ten cups of coffee and maybe eat a quick sandwich, go home and have dinner with the family as fast as possible, go into my study to finish reading my medical journals, and then, if it wasn't too late, I'd watch TV until I fell asleep. Even if I took time out for a walk in the woods behind our house, or a basketball game with the boys, I'd always be figuring out some new surgical procedure in my head. My mind was always chattering like a monkey. It took this major operation—on *my* body, for a change—to convince me that I don't want to live the rest of my life on automatic pilot. I want to learn to live in the present moment, to enjoy what I have."

Whenever a person makes this major shift in attitude, the door to real, daily-life stress management has opened. It becomes possible to learn how to follow cardiologist Dr. Robert Eliot's rule for coping with stress: "If you can't fight and you can't flee, flow."[4]

[4] C. Wallis, "Stress: We Can Cope," *Time*, June 6, 1983, p. 48.

Like a Surfer

The wisdom you can develop from the use of awareness and a self-investigative mind can lead you to a deep experience of inner relaxation. According to Joan Harrigan, Ph.D., in the article, "Meditation and the Meaning of Life":

> In accepting the inevitability of aloneness, suffering and death, one can actually be inspired and vitalized. For with risk comes excitement, and with acceptance of the challenge comes engagement in life. Then, like a surfer, one can actually be held aloft by the waves and currents that sweep others away. It all depends on *how they are perceived*.[5]

We're not promising that you'll become an "accomplished surfer." But we are pointing the way, taking you to the ocean, providing the surfboard. It will soon be time to take your first ride.

---

[5] Jean Harrigan, "Meditation and Meaning in Life," *Dawn*, 2 (1982), 35.

PART II

Preparing for the Less Stress Lessons

Finding Your Own Personal Stress Buttons

"It is not true that life is one damn thing after another—it's one damn thing over and over."

—Edna St. Vincent Millay

Most people have a tendency to live "on automatic pilot," reacting in the same way, over and over again, whenever their stress buttons are pushed. Everyday stress doesn't have to be an enemy to your well-being and health if you learn to become aware of what you find stressful in your life and to *take responsibility for how you react* to these stressors. The good news is that you have a choice. A stressful event must push your *stress buttons* to become a problem for you.

For example: You've made plans to meet your friend Dick for dinner. He's late, and as you sit and wait for him you begin to think, "I've been stood up! I'll never meet the right kind of man. God, I must be unattractive."

A second person might think, "Dick must have been in an accident. Oh, this is awful. I'd better call the police and all the hospitals."

A third person might think, "I hope Dick hasn't been caught up in traffic, but it will be good to see him when he gets here. If he's late or doesn't show up because he forgot our date, I'll talk with him about how I feel."

Obviously the third person will experience much less stress in response to the identical situation.

What kinds of events push your stress buttons? What usually makes you explode with anger or frustration, tightens your muscles into knots, or causes you to withdraw into a silent pout?

Keeping a Stress Diary

In order to analyze and understand your stress reaction patterns, we want you to keep a stress diary for at least four days. Begin to notice even the briefest moments in your life when you feel tense and uptight. Throughout the day make notes, listing stressful situations or feelings:

- What was your response or reaction when the stressful event occurred?
- What thoughts did you have before, during, and after the event?
- Did you notice any physical or emotional symptoms?
- Did you resolve the situation? If so, how?

As you keep your stress diary you may notice that you feel upset or tense or you may develop a physical symptom when there hasn't been any noticeable external event to cause these feelings or symptoms. It's important to stay aware of your mental activity—not just external events. All it takes is one thought to set off an entire chain of feelings, which can lead to a full-blown fight-or-flight reaction. It may also be helpful to note your consumption of foods containing sugar and caffeine, to see what effect they have on your body and mind.

At the end of each day look over the stressful events or thoughts and see if you can find any patterns emerging:

- What situations or thoughts usually provoke a stress reaction?
- Do certain foods provoke a stress reaction?
- What are your typical stress reactions?
- Do you experience stress in particular areas of your body, such as a knot in your stomach, tight shoulders, or sweaty palms?
- Can you see the difference between a stressful event or thought and your reaction to the event or thought?

It is essential to discover your stress reaction patterns in order to develop enough awareness to make behavioral changes.

Sally G., 34, married, mother of two, business manager of a well-known recording company

Sally has always been able to juggle her multiple roles with almost the technical skill and speed of a home computer. But lately it has seemed like something is out of sync. Sally has been unable to relax, and more and more often, she has forgotten to do essential tasks at work. Her concentration has just not been as sharp as usual, and Sally has blamed this change on her back. By the end of most workdays, Sally's lower back throbs with pain. She has seen two top specialists, both of whom have assured her that there is no organic problem. "Just stress," they each concluded after a battery of tests came back negative, and they wrote prescriptions for mild muscle relaxants. Recently Sally has even lost her sexual desire for her husband. "Everyone tells me how successful I am," Sally says, "and many of my friends envy my life. I don't know why I feel so tense and exhausted all the time."

As you can see, Sally's inability to relax is affecting many aspects of her life—her body, her work, and her marriage. She feels anxious, but she doesn't know exactly why. Keeping a stress diary for a week helped her pinpoint the causes of her tension. Here is an excerpt from Sally G.'s stress diary:

10:00 A.M.	Passed Mr. Connolly in the hall. He barely nodded. I'm sure he doesn't like me and will write a bad evaluation of my department. I perspired and my mouth felt dry.
10:45 A.M.	Felt a backache coming on. Took two aspirin.
11:20 A.M.	Hank called. He'll be late tonight. I felt scared. Everyone I know is getting divorced. Why can't we talk anymore? I couldn't concentrate on writing my report. Took a Valium at lunchtime.
2:10 P.M.	School nurse called. Suzy's got a sore throat again. Might be tonsillitis. They want me to pick her up. It was probably my fault. I was in such a rush this A.M., I didn't check to see if she was dressed warmly. Damn, I'll never get that report finished on time.
2:30 P.M.	On the way to school, got stuck behind a slowpoke and hit every red light. I know it didn't matter if I was late, but I felt so mad at the other driver, I wanted to scream. In the car, noticed my jaw was clenched, heart racing, shoulders hunched. By the time I got to school, my back started to hurt again.
3:15 P.M.	Suzy refused to take her medicine and was real sassy. I yelled at her, but it just made things worse. I don't know how to handle her sometimes. My back was throbbing, so I took a hot shower and felt a bit better. Talked to Suzy again when I felt calmer and helped her with her homework. I wish I had more time to be with her.

4:00 P.M. Mail came. National Conference people invited someone else to give the opening address, which had been my responsibility for the past three years! Felt depressed. What did I do wrong last year? Why didn't they tell me about this? Cried and felt a bit shaky. Ate a candy bar.

8:00 P.M. Hank came home. I was out in the garden and he came over to hug me. I know he felt me stiffen up, but he didn't say anything. What's wrong with me? I love him, but I no longer want to make love with him. Or even hold him. It must be two months since we had sex! I told Hank I was upset about the report at work. Decided to put in a few hours of work on it. Back aching. Had two cups of coffee.

11:00 P.M. Had trouble getting to sleep. Kept worrying about tomorrow—phone calls to make, find a baby-sitter for Saturday, Mr. Connolly, etc., etc. Will my back pain ever go away? Whole body felt tense. Took a Valium and finally fell asleep.

Today's Stress Buttons:

1. Criticism from boss. Being judged or rejected.
2. Deadlines—afraid I won't finish things on time.
3. Problems with kids. Lack of time.
4. Lots of self-judging thoughts and guilt.
5. Always in a rush.
6. Worrying about marital relationship.
7. Worrying about the next day.

Today's Stress Reactions:

1. Backache.
2. Inability to concentrate.
3. Distance from husband.

4. Irritable with Suzy.
5. Insomnia.

Now it's time for you to keep your own stress diary. As you discover your stress buttons and your patterns of reactivity to stress, be gentle and patient with yourself. You aren't keeping this diary in order to judge yourself. This is a time for self-discovery and self-understanding.

Your Less Stress Goals

Now that you have spent at least four days observing and writing down your habitual reactions to stressful situations, it's time to begin formulating some goals for the next month. In order to make changes in the ways you handle stress, first you must decide specifically what it is you wish to change. In some cases you can actually change a situation and remove the cause of the stress—for example, by finding a new job or moving out of an unhealthy environment. More often it is necessary to remain in the same situation and learn how to respond differently.

When you set your Less Stress Goals, think of them as gifts to yourself. Avoid long lists of "should's," "must's," and "ought to's," and focus instead on developing only a few changes in behavior or attitude. To find two or three changes you want to make, look over your stress diary. What stressful situations or reaction patterns seem to occur most often in your life? To come up with realistic and specific goals, consider the following guidelines:

1. Each goal should be very specific. Don't set vague goals, such as, "I want to be a kind and wonderful mother." Instead you could say, "I want to get through

two full days this month without yelling at the kids unnecessarily."

2. You should feel certain that you can make some noticeable progress on each goal in approximately thirty days.
3. Each goal should reflect something *you* really want to change about your behavior or your attitude, *not* something a family member wants you to change (unless they coincide).
4. The *process* of working on each goal should be as important to you as accomplishing the goal. In other words, you should be able to learn something valuable from simply attempting to make this change.
5. Each goal should be flexible. You can change it, but try to set fairly easy, straightforward goals to begin with.

Jim B., 18, single, college freshman

Jim is the first person in his family to go to college, and he feels a lot of pressure to do well. But Jim is having a difficult time managing all his schoolwork. He's heading for an engineering major and finds that all his courses are demanding and time-consuming. He gets overwhelmed, procrastinates, feels perpetually unprepared, and then panics on exams.

Also, Jim has started drinking heavily, particularly at parties. "I walk into a party feeling really psyched, then I see a good-looking woman and I lose it. I can't think of a thing to say. But after some beers nothing matters—until the next day when I'm too sick to study."

Jim's list of goals might look like this:

1. I want to manage my study time better so I can complete all my papers one week before midterms.
2. I want to learn how to relax at parties and on dates without having more than one drink.

3. I want to be less judgmental when I make mistakes on tests.

Now take some time to reflect. Look over your stress diary notes, then write down two or three goals for this coming month right here in this book:

Your Less Stress Goals

1. ______________________________

____

2. ______________________________

____

3. ______________________________

____

As you begin your daily Less Stress Lessons remember to reread your goals every day. Although each lesson may not apply specifically to your goals, you will be learning to respond in a healthier manner to many of the stressful situations in your life. Awareness of your specific goals can be your key to beginning this work. As you do the Less Stress Lessons you may wish to change, rewrite, or adapt these goals. Feel free to use them in any way that is helpful to you.

Nutrition, Exercise, and Stress

Margery A., 27, married, graduate student in public health and part-time family planning counselor

Margery's schedule sometimes feels overwhelming. On a typical day she gets up at 7:00 A.M., frequently after only five or six hours of sleep, dresses quickly, and leaves for an 8:00 A.M. class, stopping at the deli for a cheese danish and a large coffee on her way to class. She grabs another coffee on her way to the office after class and works through her lunch break, stopping briefly to eat a bagel. She munches on corn chips all afternoon. By 4:00 P.M. she's had five cups of coffee and complains that her stomach is queasy. She has a seminar from 4:30 to 7:00 P.M. and eats a candy bar just before class to give her some energy. She meets her husband after class. They're both too tired and rushed to cook, so they go out for a pizza. Margery feels very tense, so she orders a pina colada, which makes her feel sleepy. She has to stay up late preparing for her statistics class, so she has another cup of coffee. She finally gets to bed at midnight but can't fall asleep.

Periodically, Margery says to her husband, "We've got to start eating better. We're spending too much money, and I've gained ten pounds since I started graduate school." But they're always too busy to shop or cook.

Margery's eating habits not only strain her budget and increase her weight, they also contribute to her feeling of stress. In the first place, she's not eating a balanced diet.

An occasional day like the one described won't hurt you, but a consistent high-fat, high-sugar, fast-food diet could have long-term negative effects on your overall health and ability to resist the effects of stress.

In the short term, Margery is caught in a common stress-producing cycle. There's too much to do and not enough time; she doesn't get enough sleep; she's exhausted and thus turns to caffeine and sugar for quick energy. But the caffeine and sugar are stressors themselves. By the end of the day she's jangled and jittery and, once again, can't sleep.

With a little time and planning Margery could make a significant impact on her stress level. She needs to stay as healthy as possible, and this means eating a well-balanced diet. It also means scheduling time for regular exercise. A half hour a day of stretching or aerobic exercise—running, biking, swimming, brisk walking—would both ease the tension in tight muscles and increase her energy. And she wouldn't feel as tense at the end of the day.

Nutrition and exercise are an important part of stress management. We are not nutritionists or exercise scientists and can only give commonsense advice. But we encourage you to consult our bibliography or experts in your local area.

Sex and Stress

Using this book will probably not be enough to help anyone solve serious and persistent sexual problems, such as painful intercourse, fear of intimacy, long-term impotency, or the inability to have an orgasm. In these cases, it's best to see a professional therapist.

However, many sexual problems are directly related to

the inability to relax. Sexual desire doesn't have much chance to awaken if your mind is cluttered with worried thoughts, or if your body is tense and tight.

To feel free and uninhibited sexually, you must first trust your partner. Then you must relax enough to be able to experience the sensations in each moment.

As you practice the Less Stress Lessons you may notice that your ability to experience and enjoy your sexuality will increase as your tension levels decrease.

Be sure to read some of the books in our reference list if this is an area of stress or concern in your life.

Time Management

Time management is another crucial part of stress management. One of the most common complaints we hear is, "But I don't have time to relax." If this sounds like a familiar statement, we have some ideas that might help you.

There are two ways to approach time management. One way is through life planning—a method of setting long- and short-term goals, then planning how to achieve them. Life planning is beyond the scope of this book, but check the bibliography at the end for references.

We're going to focus here on how to manage your day-to-day schedule so you have more time to take care of yourself and to practice the Less Stress Lessons.

The keys to effective daily time management are making lists, setting priorities, and using schedules.

1. Make a list of everything you need or want to do in the next few days. Include entertainment and relaxation.
2. Go through the list and put a number 1 next to every-

thing that is top priority—i.e., that absolutely has to be done, and/or is essential to your well-being. Then indicate medium-priority items (important but not essential) with a number 2 and then low-priority items (not really important) with a number 3.

3. Using a blank sheet of paper or a schedule book, write down all appointments and commitments for the next few days. Be sure to include work hours, travel time, and mealtimes.
   - Where do you have blocks of free time?
   - Are all top-priority items already accounted for in your schedule?
   - If not, where can you fit them in?
   - If you have no extra time, review your schedule. How much of your time is given to top-priority items? Medium-priority? Low-priority?
   - Can you spend less time on, or eliminate, medium- and low-priority items?
   - Have you classified everything as top-priority?

People frequently have difficulty with time management. Time management techniques are practical, commonsense ideas, but they bring up lots of resistance and "yes, but's." If you hear yourself saying, "I'd love to practice the Less Stress Lessons, but I don't have fifteen minutes to spare," we ask you to challenge yourself. If you're concerned about your stress level, if you've bought this book and taken the time to read this far, then chances are that stress management is top-priority. Be creative, reevaluate your priorities, and ask for help. Maybe you need to get up earlier. "What an awful idea," you say, but remember, we're only asking for fifteen minutes, and you'll end up with more energy and *less stress*.

PART III

The Less Stress Daily Lessons

The Less Stress Daily Lessons

Try to do the Less Stress Lessons every day. Each day you will be learning new ways in which to help yourself develop awareness and manage stress. Read over each daily lesson carefully, *two* or *three* times, and then try the exercise for yourself. It might help to tape record the instructions so you can listen to them. Don't just read through the lessons. Do them! Doing them will lead you to the changes you want to make in your life.

Each lesson consists of one exercise to practice once or twice that day, several assignments to do during the day, and a helpful thought to focus on. Even if a lesson doesn't seem to relate specifically to your stress problems, try it anyway. Each exercise will give you the opportunity to learn something new about yourself.

If you miss a day, just begin again wherever you left off. You may also choose to repeat any lesson for as many days as you want before continuing to the next Less Stress Lesson. You might even want to work with a lesson for a week or more at a time. Trust your own rhythms and needs, and keep going at your own pace. If you have any difficulty doing a lesson, don't just give up. It may take a few days of practice to feel the benefits of a new technique or approach. Be patient and try the lesson a few times, but if you still feel no benefit, don't worry. Just go on to the next lesson. Each person will find certain exercises that are especially beneficial and useful for them.

Get ready to start. Remember, this important work will

require only fifteen minutes of your day. Find a quiet space in your house or office in which to do the exercises. Later on, you'll be able to do many of these exercises in the middle of Madison Square Garden, but make it easy on yourself at first. Choose a time of day to practice relaxation when you have fifteen minutes to be alone, when you can take the phone off the hook or have someone else answer it for you. Having read the section on time management, you'll be able to find the time to do these exercises.

Tell your family members, roommates, or officemates that you need some support. Ask them to help you by being quiet when you are practicing the exercises. At first they may complain. People are used to you just the way you are, and any change can be stressful and threatening to *them*. But when they begin to see the positive changes you make, they might even want to join you. We certainly encourage you to do the lessons together with a friend or family member, but don't try to convince or force anyone to join you in the Less Stress Program. You can only be responsible for changing yourself!

The Less Stress Lessons are going to ask you to pay a lot of attention to yourself. Many of you spend a great deal of your lives meeting other people's demands, so learning to take time for yourself will be extremely important. As your energy increases and you have more control over your life, you will be able to help other people when it is appropriate *and* continue to take good care of yourself. To be of service to others can be an invaluable way to maintain perspective on your life, but now it's time to be of service to yourself first.

The Less Stress Program is just the beginning of a lifetime of increasing self-awareness. No one can achieve inner peace in a short time, but the Less Stress Lessons will help you begin the journey. Remember that learning to play an instrument can be uncomfortable at first. It takes regular practice and commitment to become good enough to improvise. While doing these lessons *you* will be your own instrument. Practice. Be patient. Enjoy yourself. You are on your way to being able to live with the wisdom expressed in the Serenity Prayer:

> Give me the serenity to accept the things I cannot change,
> The courage to change the things I can,
> And the wisdom to know the difference.

Instructions

1. If possible, read each lesson first thing in the morning, even if you can't do the exercise until later in the day.
2. You can do each exercise with your eyes open or closed. Some people find it easier to do the exercises with their eyes closed. If you wear contact lenses, you might wish to remove them before beginning.
3. Loosen any tight clothing—belts, waistbands—before beginning the practice period. You want to be as comfortable as possible when you are doing the exercises.
4. If you lie down, make sure you are lying on a pad, carpet, or mattress that is comfortable and provides back support. If you sit down, make sure the chair is comfortable and supports your back.
5. Before going to bed, take a few minutes to review the day's lesson.

Lesson 1: Body Scan

"The more we accept of ourselves, the more fully we experience the world."

—Stephen Levine

In order to learn how to relax, you first must discover where, when, and how you store tension in your body.

Body Scan Exercise

1. Lie down or sit comfortably, without slumping. Loosen your clothing. Uncross your arms and legs, and close your eyes if you wish.
2. Begin to mentally scan the sensations in your body, starting with your toes. Do you feel:
   - tension
   - relaxation
   - warmth
   - coolness
   - hardness
   - softness
   - lack of any sensation?
3. Very slowly, on the *left* side of your body, start scanning your ankle, calf, lower leg, knee, thigh, and hip. What do you feel in each area?
4. Repeat on your *right* side.
5. Notice if one side of your body feels different from the other side. If so, how?
   - Is one side more tense and tight than the other?

- Do you feel more sensation on one side?
- Is one side warmer?

6. Now scan your genital and pelvic areas, inner thighs, buttocks, abdomen, chest, lower back, up the spinal column, shoulder area, and neck. What do you feel in each area?
7. Slowly move your neck from side to side. Notice where the movement feels free and loose and where it feels tight or painful. Do you notice any knots of tension in the neck area?
8. Pay attention to your facial muscles, noting:
   - jaw area tension or relaxation
   - forehead
   - the area around your eyes
   - your tongue
   - your temples
   - your scalp.
9. Scan your body again, slowly moving your attention from your head down to your toes. Does your body feel any different now? How?
   - more relaxed
   - softer
   - warmer
   - colder?
10. Are you more aware of the places where you store tension? If so, where?
    - legs
    - pelvic area
    - stomach
    - chest
    - back
    - shoulders
    - face
    - chest?
11. Take in a few nice deep breaths. Wiggle and stretch your arms and legs. Slowly open your eyes, if they were closed, and continue with the day.

Assignments

1. Do this Body Scan Exercise for five to ten minutes, once or twice today.
2. Several times today, stop what you are doing—and do a quick, eyes-open version of the body scan, mentally checking out your tension levels. You can do this when you are sitting, walking, driving, waiting on line, talking to others, or even while exercising.
3. Review your Less Stress Goals on page 36.

Lesson 2: The Natural Diaphragmatic Breath

"Our breath is the bridge from our body to our mind."
—Thich Nhat Hanh

Most people in the Western world have forgotten the natural, full breathing they did as infants—when the abdomen moved up and down with each breath, indicating the internal movement of the diaphragm. Westerners are only beginning to recognize the health benefits of correct breathing.

Over the centuries, various breathing exercises have been used as an integral part of physical, mental, and spiritual development in many Asian cultures and religions. Phil Nuernberger, Ph.D., stress researcher and author of *Freedom from Stress,* says:

> Through experimentation and study, advanced yogis have explored this complex area and have recognized and verified that the breath is the key mediating factor between mind and body. . . . Because of its unique relationship to the autonomic nervous system, the breath plays a vital role in determining whether or not we suffer from stress. Whichever way one breathes, there is no difference in the amount of oxygen consumed by the body, but there is a vast difference in the amount of work required by the lungs and heart to accomplish the same amount of oxygenation. In fact, the workload of the cardiopulmonary system may be reduced by as much as 50% by changing from Thoracic (chest) to Diaphragmatic (belly) breathing. . . . Our breathing patterns and our emotional and physical states are intimately interrelated. Each affects and is affected by the other. . . . As emotional imbalance disturbs

the breathing patterns, shallow and jerky breathing also disturbs the mind. And when the mind is disturbed, the biochemistry is also affected.[6]

Thoracic, or chest breathing is related directly to the activation of the fight-or-flight arousal mechanism. By training yourself to breathe naturally and diaphragmatically, you may be able to prevent some stress reactivity and learn to return more quickly to a balanced state after a stress reaction.

Besides the physiological benefits, we believe that there is another major advantage to using awareness of the breath as a primary method of relaxation training: as long as you are alive, you will be breathing. Each time you bring your awareness back to your breathing, you come back into the present moment. You are alive. You are breathing. Now. This moment.

During the first week of Less Stress Lessons you will learn many breathing exercises. These will be your first tools to help develop your ability to relax more deeply.

Diaphragmatic Breath Exercise

1. Lie down or sit comfortably with your spine fairly straight. Place one hand on your abdomen. Close your eyes if you wish.
2. Bring your awareness to your breathing and mentally follow the sensations as you breathe. Notice if you breathe through your mouth or your nose. Don't exaggerate your normal breathing or try to control it in any way. Just be aware of the natural flow of your breath. Don't strain or consciously try to take very deep breaths. Is your breathing:

---

[6] Phil Nuernberger, *Freedom from Stress: A Holistic Approach* (Honesdale, PA: Himalayan Institute, 1981), p. 173.

- shallow
- deep
- fast
- slow
- rhythmic
- jerky?

3. Pay attention to the sensations of air coming in and out of your nose or mouth. Follow its path as it enters your body, goes down into your chest and abdomen, and as it releases upon exhalation. Feel your back and abdomen, and then your chest, expand gently as you breathe in and release as you breathe out.
4. Bring your attention specifically to your abdomen and see if you can feel it rise a little bit as you inhale and fall as you exhale. Your hand will rise and fall with the rhythm of your breathing.

   If you find it too difficult to breathe into your abdomen, just observe your normal breath. Don't force it or strain. The abdomen will move only slightly if you are breathing diaphragmatically.

   If you feel light-headed, this means that you are forcing yourself to breathe too deeply. The diaphragmatic breath is a natural breath, not an exaggeratedly deep breath. Pay attention to the sensations you feel as you breathe.
5. Continue with the awareness of breathing for five to ten minutes. Notice if your pattern of breathing changes at all. Does it become:
   - deeper
   - slower
   - more rhythmic?

If your mind wanders, simply return to the awareness of your breathing. It is normal for the mind to travel to the past or the future. Keep coming back to the present moment. This breath. Right now.

6. When you feel ready, take in two or three nice, deep breaths. Wiggle your toes and fingers; stretch your arms and legs. If your eyes are closed, open them slowly. Take your time before standing up. Continue with the day, feeling refreshed and alert. (If you do this exercise before bedtime, just continue to relax as long as you wish by staying aware of the breath and allow the relaxation to lead you to a deep sleep.)

Assignments

1. Do the Diaphragmatic Breathing Exercise for ten minutes or more, once or twice today. Observe whether your breathing patterns change as your emotional states change during the day. If you are under stress, concentrate on breathing diaphragmatically for a few moments. Notice whether there is any change in your feelings.
2. Continue doing the brief Body Scan throughout the day —at home, at work, in the car.
3. Review your Less Stress Goals.

Lesson 3: Body Scan and Diaphragmatic Breathing

"Breathing is a remarkable phenomenon. In breathing, man copies the rhythm of the universe."
—*Timothy Gallwey*

In today's lesson you will combine the two methods you have already learned. As you become aware of tense areas in your body, you can use the breath to release and soften this tension.

Gloria T., 44, divorced, social worker

Gloria had studied for her social work certification exam for weeks. This was a very important test—Gloria needed to pass it in order to advance to the type of job and salary she wanted. When she was driving to the test site, she noticed that she was clutching the steering wheel with all her might, clenching her jaw, and taking very quick, shallow breaths. When she parked her car, Gloria scanned her body again and did a few minutes of diaphragmatic breathing. Gloria knew that the more relaxed she was, the better her concentration would be. Throughout the test she periodically checked her bodily tension levels and took some diaphragmatic breaths to relax. The test was difficult, but when Gloria left, she knew she had done the best she could on it.

You will find that you can use this technique in hundreds of situations during the day.

Body Scan and Diaphragmatic Breathing Exercise

1. Lie down or sit comfortably. Close your eyes if you wish. Take several minutes to scan your body for areas of tension.

   Concentrate on your natural breathing pattern for a few minutes.

   Concentrate on diaphragmatic breathing for a few minutes.
2. Scan your body again, noting if anything has changed.
   - Do you feel more relaxed?
   - Are you more aware of areas of tension?
3. Choose one area in your body where you still feel some tension. Imagine, when you inhale, that your breath goes directly to the area of tension. Imagine the tight muscles in that area letting go, feeling loose and warm as you exhale. Allow the breath to relax you naturally from the inside out—as though the breath is giving your muscles an internal massage.

   Continue to breathe naturally and diaphragmatically. Imagine your breath as a stream of warm air that caresses your tight muscles, replacing tension with relaxation.
4. Scan your body again, noting if anything has changed. Does any part of your body feel:
   - warm
   - light
   - large
   - heavy
   - loose?

5. When you feel ready, take a few deep, energizing breaths. Fill your lungs and sigh out on the exhales. Ahh . . .

   Stretch, open your eyes (if they were closed), and continue with the day.

Assignments

1. Do the Body Scan and Diaphragmatic Breathing Exercise for ten minutes, once or twice today.
2. Continue doing the brief Body Scan throughout the day. In addition, do at least ten seconds of diaphragmatic breathing after each body scan.

   Pay attention to your breathing patterns during the day, especially during stressful times. Are you breathing into your abdomen or just into your chest?
3. Review your Less Stress Goals.

Lesson 4: The Calm and Regular Breath

"Every situation, properly perceived, becomes an opportunity to heal."

—A Course in Miracles

Research has shown that the silent repetition of a phrase can lead to deep levels of physiological relaxation. This exercise can make it easier for you to concentrate and to stay aware of each breath as it comes in and goes out.

David J., 37, single, advertising executive

David has an explosive temper and has lost several clients and relationships over the years due to his inappropriate outbursts. When he did his stress diary, he discovered that being criticized was his most common stress button. He hated to admit he was wrong. Since David wanted to change this destructive pattern—in fact, it was one of his Less Stress goals—he began to pay attention to his breathing whenever someone criticized him. He learned that rapid chest breathing was an early warning sign of a coming explosion. Now, as soon as he notices that his breathing is irregular, David begins to repeat the phrase "My breath is calm and regular" to himself. He has been able to prevent himself from having a temper tantrum several times already.

As you will see, you can use this exercise to help you calm down even in the midst of stressful situations.

Calm and Regular Breath Exercise

1. Lie down or sit comfortably. Close your eyes if you wish.

   Do a quick Body Scan to find out how you are feeling right now. Pay attention to:
   - your posture
   - tense areas
   - areas of relaxation.
2. Pay attention to your breathing, especially to the sensations of the rising and falling of your abdomen.

   As you feel your breath becoming more and more steady, say to yourself silently, in your mind, "My breath feels calm and regular . . . calm and regular . . . calm and regular. . . ." Repeat this phrase over and over again, as slowly as you wish.

   Feel your breathing as it becomes more and more calm, more and more regular.
3. Whenever you notice that your mind has wandered, gently return to the awareness of the breath and the silent repetition of the phrase.

   After a few minutes of repetition let the phrase drop away. Continue to concentrate on the sensations of breathing for a few more minutes.
4. Scan your body again. If there are any areas of tension that need extra attention, use your imagination to send your breath right into those areas, like a gentle inner massage.
5. Take in a few nice, deep breaths. Wiggle and stretch your arms and legs. When you are ready, open your eyes (if they are closed) and continue with your day.

Assignments

1. Do the Calm and Regular Breath Exercise once or twice today.
   During the day, try silently repeating this phrase for up to thirty seconds as you pay attention to your breathing.
2. Continue doing the quick Body Scan and Diaphragmatic Breathing exercises throughout the day.
   Pay attention to your breathing patterns, particularly during stressful situations, throughout the day.
3. Review your Less Stress Goals.

Lesson 5:
The Energizing Breath

"A person who knows how to breathe is a person who knows how to build up endless vitality."

—Thich Nhat Hanh

With every breath you take, oxygen fills and revitalizes every single cell in your body. This lesson will help you begin to actually feel this internal process. By using your imagination, you can send your breath directly into areas of your body that feel dull, sluggish, or tense. As you bring your awareness into these areas, you may be able to feel the renewal of energy as your body relaxes.

Jean-Jacques P., 89, widower, vineyard owner in France

Jean-Jacques is a physically fit, mentally active senior citizen. He begins every morning with deep, energizing breaths. "What a delicious feeling. I savor the air, like some people savor my wine," he says.

Energizing Breath Exercise

1. Stand up or sit down, and close your eyes if you wish.
2. Take a deep breath in and feel your abdomen expand as

you bring your arms out to your sides and slowly up over your head. Stretch.

3. As you breathe in, imagine that you are breathing in energy and vitality to your entire body. . . . Imagine that your body feels more alive, that increased energy is spreading through every part of your body.

   Notice any sensations you feel, such as:
   - tingling
   - warmth
   - relaxation.
4. On the exhalation slowly release the air from your lungs as you bring your arms down to your sides. Repeat this sequence three times.
5. Now focus on one area where you feel tension, such as a tight shoulder muscle. Take an energizing breath and imagine your breath moving right into the knotted-up muscles at the base of your neck and down into the shoulder blade. Imagine your warm breath massaging those muscles. Feel the tension dissolve. Exhale.

   Choose another area of your body to focus on, and use your breath to energize this area.
6. Now, as you breathe in and out, imagine or actually feel pleasant sensations flowing through your entire body. Your body may feel:
   - warm
   - light
   - tingling
   - loose.

   Imagine that the breath becomes a waterfall, surrounding and filling your body with energy, and washing away the tension.
7. Take in a few extra deep breaths and make an audible sigh on each exhale. Ahhhh . . .

   Stretch slowly. With your hands reaching up to the ceiling, rock your entire body side to side by switching your weight from your left foot to your right. Slowly, let your arms come down to your sides. Stand still for a few moments. Let your eyes open (if they were closed), and enjoy the sights and colors around you.

8. Begin the next moment of your life feeling refreshed and energized.

Assignments

1. Do the Energizing Breath Exercise at least once today, for five to ten minutes.

   Take a few energizing breaths during the day—in the car, at work, or at home.
2. Continue to use your quick Body Scan and Diaphragmatic Breathing exercises throughout the day. Pay attention to your breathing patterns, particularly during stressful times, throughout the day.
3. Review your Less Stress Goals.

Lesson 6: Progressive Relaxation —Quick Procedure

"Patience is needed with everyone, but first of all with ourselves."

—*St. Francis de Sales*

Learning to control muscle tension is the basis of an effective and widely used relaxation method described by Edmond Jacobsen, M.D., in 1929. He found that it was easier to relax a muscle group by tensing it first, and then experiencing relaxation in contrast to the tension. This method depends on systematically tensing and relaxing every muscle group in our body.

Most people aren't aware of which of their muscles are chronically tense; however, you have been practicing the Body Scan for almost a week, and probably you have a pretty good picture of where your bodily tension is stored. In the next lesson you will work on all of your major muscle groups:

- Feet, thighs, buttocks, and calves
- Chest, stomach, and lower back
- Head, face, throat, neck, and shoulders
- Hands, forearms, and biceps.

Each muscle area will be tensed for five to ten seconds and

then relaxed for twenty to thirty seconds. Then you will repeat the exercise at least once for each muscle group.

If you've recently injured a muscle, be careful not to tighten it too much. If you need to, just skip it. With shoulders and feet, muscle cramping is common during the tensing of the muscles. Be careful not to strain as you tighten these muscles. Stay aware of the major and minor differences you feel between tension and relaxation.

Al R., 48, married, manager at a large corporation

Al uses progressive relaxation each day to help him deal with the heavy work responsibilities at his busy office. Managing so many people—with all their varied personality quirks—can be quite a strain, and Al is the type to bottle up his feelings. Al had been diagnosed with moderately high blood pressure, but he was unhappy about the prospect of taking medications because of their unpleasant side effects. With his doctor's approval Al decided to go on the Less Stress Program to see if he could lower his blood pressure on his own. He does his daily relaxation practice in a small computer storage room at work, and by the time he finishes his period of progressive relaxation, he feels calmer and better able to deal with the problems on the job. Both Al and his doctor feel optimistic: already, after some practice, Al's blood pressure has begun to drop.

Progressive Relaxation Exercise

1. Sit or lie down in a comfortable position. Close your eyes if you wish.
2. Pull your toes back toward your face and tighten your shins. Hold this and feel the tension for five to ten seconds.

   Let go and relax for twenty to thirty seconds. Notice

the differences between tension and relaxation. Repeat this sequence at least once.

3. Now point your toes downward as you tighten calves, thighs, and buttocks. Hold for five to ten seconds. Let go and relax for twenty or thirty seconds. Repeat this sequence at least once.

   Feel the waves of relaxation moving through your lower body.
4. Take a deep breath in and arch your back slightly while pressing your stomach out. Hold for five to ten seconds. Let go and relax for twenty to thirty seconds. Feel the difference. Repeat.
5. Hunch your shoulders forward and up toward your ears. At the same time wrinkle up the muscles of your face like a prune. Hold. Let go and relax. Feel the difference. Repeat.

   Feel the waves of muscular relaxation moving throughout your entire body.

Assignments

1. Do the Progressive Relaxation exercise once or twice today.
2. Use segments of the Progressive Relaxation Exercise during your day to help you relax your body whenever you notice tension developing in your muscles. You can try tightening and relaxing just one muscle area, such as your hands.
3. Continue with the quick Body Scan and Diaphragmatic Breathing exercises throughout the day.

   Pay attention to your breathing patterns, especially during stressful situations, throughout the day.
4. Review your Less Stress Goals.

Lesson 7: Gentle Stretching

"A garden gate that does not swing gets rusty in the hinges. Our bodies do the same!"

—Dr. Turner

By doing a series of gentle stretching exercises while breathing rhythmically and diaphragmatically, by slowing down your movements, and by paying attention every moment to the sensations you feel as you stretch, you can relax, energize, and strengthen your body. Through slow, gentle stretching your tight and tense muscles become looser and more flexible.

In the following two lessons we have chosen some very simple stretches. You can also apply this method of slow, attentive stretching to any physical exercises you already know and practice. Most of you should have no trouble doing these lessons, but if you have physical problems that prevent you from doing the stretching, just repeat any previous lesson.

Gentle Stretching Exercise

1. If you like, put on some slow instrumental music. Sit or stand up. Close your eyes if you wish.
2. Breathe in as you bring your right arm out to your side and raise it up over your head. Breathe out. Breathe in as you stretch your right arm up toward the ceiling, as if

you were stretching for an apple at the top of a tree. Breathe out.

Then, breathing in, stretch your left arm up in the same fashion. Breathe out.

Let both your arms come down slowly as you breathe out. Feel the release of tension as you continue to breathe diaphragmatically for about twenty seconds.

3. Place your feet shoulder-width apart. Slowly, with awareness, let your head hang forward, your chin reaching for or touching your chest.

   Begin to curl slowly forward, bending down one vertebra at a time. Keep breathing. Hang down only as far as is comfortable for you. *Don't strain!* If you are standing, let your knees bend.

   Gently sway from side to side, as if a gentle breeze were blowing. *Don't* bounce up and down.

   Continue breathing diaphragmatically throughout this exercise and come to rest in this position.

   On each inhale, come back up a little bit. On each exhale, rest. In this way, slowly roll your body back up until your spine is straight and your head is resting in a balanced position. Pay attention to each sensation you feel during these movements.

   Notice how your body feels. Is it:
   - tight
   - sore
   - relaxed
   - loose
4. Relax for a minute or more, noticing how you feel by scanning your body mentally.
   - Do you feel looser? More relaxed?
   - Is any area still tight?

Assignments

1. Practice the Gentle Stretching Exercise once today for about ten minutes—or use your own exercise routine in this slow, attentive way.

   Try stretching during the day, especially if you feel any tension in your body or mind.
2. Continue using the quick Body Scan and Diaphragmatic Breathing throughout the day.

   Pay attention to your breathing patterns, especially during stressful situations, throughout the day.

   Use your choice of relaxation techniques throughout the day.
3. Review your Less Stress Goals.

Lesson 8: Gentle Stretching, Part II

"You have only one life. Live it with a body in good physical condition."

—Ruth Bender

Today you will continue with the gentle stretching. Remember, the emphasis in this exercise is on slowing down your movements and paying attention to each movement and sensation.

Gentle Stretching Exercise

1. If you prefer, put on some slow instrumental music.

   Lie down on your back with your arms at your sides on an exercise mat, blanket, or soft rug. Close your eyes, if you wish. Pay attention to your movements as you get into this posture. Move slowly, with awareness.
2. Slowly raise your knees, allowing them to bend but with your feet still resting on the mat or floor.

   Inhale as you raise both knees up toward your chest, letting your feet come off the floor. Press your knees down gently to your chest by reaching slowly with your hands and hugging your knees. Exhale. Keep breathing diaphragmatically as you hold this posture for twenty seconds or longer.

   Still hugging your knees to your chest, gently rock

your body from side to side as you continue breathing naturally, massaging your spine and back. When you are ready, let the movement slowly come to rest and take in a nice, deep breath.

On the exhalation, release your knees and put your feet slowly back down into the bent-knee position.

Repeat this entire sequence one more time.

3. Now begin to relax your entire body by using the Diaphragmatic Breathing Exercise. Feel your abdomen as you breathe in and out—as it rises and falls along with the rhythm of your breathing.
4. When you feel ready, stretch and take a few deeper breaths. Feel the energy and alertness filling your body.

   Stretch your entire body again. Now slowly roll over to one side, and with awareness of each movement and sensation, come slowly back up to a standing position. Take your time, there's no rush!
5. Scan your body and see how you are feeling.
   - What are your breathing patterns?
   - Is any part of your body looser? warmer? lighter? heavier?

Assignments

1. Practice the Gentle Stretching, Part II Exercise once today—or use your own exercise routine in this slow, attentive way.

   Try stretching during the day, especially if you notice any tension in your body or mind.
2. Continue to use the quick Body Scan and Diaphragmatic Breathing throughout the day.

   Pay attention to your breathing patterns, especially during stressful situations, and continue using your choice of relaxation techniques throughout the day.
3. Review your Less Stress Goals.

Lesson 9: Triggers to Relaxation

"A total immersion in life offers the best classroom for learning to love."

—Leo Buscaglia

In order to become extremely familiar and comfortable with your new relaxation skills, you need daily reminders to practice these techniques throughout your day. We call these reminders *triggers to relaxation.*

You will pick certain of your most common activities, events, or situations. These will be your triggers to relaxation. For example:

- Every time you get into your car
- Every time you hit a red light
- Every time you look at your watch
- Every time you sit down
- Every time you hang up the phone.

Each time your trigger occurs, it will serve as a reminder to practice your choice of relaxation exercises. You have many to choose from now: quick Body Scan, any of the breathing exercises, any segment of the Progressive Relaxation Exercise, or Gentle Stretching. Try using a variety of your favorite techniques throughout the day.

Triggers to Relaxation Exercise

1. Pick a few of your most common activities as triggers to relaxation.
2. Each time today when your trigger occurs, use any relaxation technique you choose for at least ten seconds.
3. Go on with your day, feeling refreshed and alert.

Assignments

1. Do the Triggers to Relaxation Exercise around twenty times today.
2. Once today, do your choice of Lessons 1 through 8 for approximately ten minutes.
3. Continue using the quick Body Scan and Diaphragmatic Breathing exercises throughout the day.
4. Review your Less Stress Goals.

Lesson 10: Visualization

"Live in each season as it passes; breathe the air, drink the drink, taste the fruit . . . be blown on by all the winds."

—Henry David Thoreau

The use of your imagination is a very powerful stress-management tool. In this lesson you will learn to create clear stress-reducing images in your mind's eye.

You can reduce your stress throughout the day by learning to picture a peaceful, relaxing image in your mind. You can use your imagination to see a situation more objectively and to try out new modes of behavior. You will learn more about this in Lessons 11 and 12.

Visualization is sometimes used to help a person change something in their body. A patient may be taught consciously to create mental images in order to heal certain symptoms or diseases or to lose or gain weight. It is very difficult to prove the effectiveness of visualization conclusively, but the anecdotal evidence can be quite persuasive. If you are interested in pursuing this idea, see our bibliography listings under "Visualization."

If you have difficulty seeing an image in your mind's eye, don't worry. You can simply think about the image instead of trying to see it.

Visualization Exercise

1. You may choose to put on soothing music. Sit or lie down, and close your eyes.

Take a few minutes to relax using your favorite relaxation technique (breathing awareness, progressive relaxation, gentle stretching).

2. Remember or imagine a beautiful place where you can feel relaxed and at peace.

   Imagine yourself in this setting. Using all your senses, experience the imagined surroundings.

   - What do you smell? Flowers? Freshly cut grass? Pines? Salt air? Experience the smells.
   - What do you hear? Birds? Wind in the trees? Waves? People's voices? Listen to the sounds.
   - What do you feel? Warmth from the sun? Cool breezes? Moisture? Grass, rocks, sand? Feel the sensations.
   - What do you see? Look around you slowly and absorb the textures, colors, shadows, movement. Experience the sights.

3. Continue relaxing for a few minutes. Let go of the images. Stretch slowly and open your eyes.

Assignments

1. Take ten to fifteen minutes to complete today's Visualization Exercise.

   Several times today, stop and mentally return to your favorite place. Experience this peaceful place fully for a few seconds or minutes.

2. Continue using your triggers to relaxation with your favorite relaxation techniques. Use the quick Body Scan and Diaphragmatic Breathing, especially during stressful situations, and pay attention to your breathing patterns throughout the day.
3. Continue using your choice of relaxation techniques (including visualization) throughout the day.
4. Review your Less Stress Goals.

Lesson 11: Image Rehearsal of Stressful Events

"Do not be too timid about your actions. All life is an experiment. The more experiments you make, the better."

—Ralph Waldo Emerson

You can reduce your stress by rehearsing an anticipated stressful event. You do this, anyway, and call it worrying about something. Image rehearsal, another valuable use for visualization, helps you take control of this worrying process so that it works for you rather than against you. By using image rehearsal, you can practice handling a potentially stressful event in a less stressful way.

Shawna M., 28, single, assistant director of the personnel department for a large computer company

Shawna was terrified of the monthly staff meetings whenever she was responsible for giving an oral presentation detailing the new programs in her department. During these talks, Shawna's lips got very dry, her knees shook, and her voice wavered quite noticeably. She was well respected in the company, but it bothered her that she felt and acted so nervous—especially in front of people she already knew. What would happen, she wondered, if she ever had to give a report at the national convention?

By using image rehearsal, Shawna was able to practice giving her monthly talk in her imagination. She used relaxation techniques to calm down, then pictured herself giving the talk with less tension and more self-confidence. Ten minutes before she actually gave her next talk, she went into the ladies' room and spent a few minutes using the Calm and Regular Breath Exercise, followed by a brief image rehearsal. On stage, right before she began to speak, Shawna took a few diaphragmatic breaths. During the talk she remembered to pay attention to her breathing and to breathe down into her abdomen.

After it was all over she said, "I still felt nervous, but the edge was off. Deep inside me, somehow, I knew I could do well—and I did. My voice seemed steadier and clearer. I have a feeling that if I keep working with image rehearsal, my fear of public speaking will gradually diminish."

Image Rehearsal of Stressful Events Exercise

1. Take a few minutes to relax using your favorite relaxation technique. Close your eyes if you wish.
2. Visualize an anticipated stressor. See the situation clearly.
   - Who is with you? Are you alone?
   - What room are you in?
   - How do you feel?
   - How do you act?
   - What are you thinking about?
   - How does your body feel?
3. Practice your relaxation technique again.

   Visualize the stressful event again.

   Imagine several new ways of feeling and acting during this event.

   Imagine yourself feeling calm and confident, before, during, and after the event.

4. Let go of the images. Relax for a few more minutes. Stretch. Open your eyes slowly and go on with your life.

Assignments

1. Take ten to fifteen minutes to complete the Image Rehearsal Exercise.

   If you have a stressful event coming up soon, practice a quick version of the Image Rehearsal Exercise before you go to sleep tonight, immediately after waking up tomorrow, and just before the actual event.
2. Continue using your triggers to relaxation, along with your favorite relaxation techniques.

   Use the quick Body Scan and Diaphragmatic Breathing throughout the day. Pay attention to your breathing patterns, especially during stressful situations, throughout the day.
3. Review your Less Stress Goals.

Lesson 12: Image Rehearsal—During and After a Stressful Event

"We should treat our anxiety, our pain, our hatred, and passion gently, respectfully, not resisting it, but living with it, making peace with it, penetrating into its nature."

—*Thich Nhat Hanh*

In the preceding lessons you have learned and practiced a variety of relaxation techniques. In Lesson 11 you had a chance to imagine yourself using these techniques to prepare yourself for stressful situations you could anticipate.

What about those unexpected stressful events? Increased familiarity with all of the relaxation techniques will allow you to choose more easily an appropriate technique even in the midst of a crisis.

Debby R., 37, married, new mother, television producer on leave of absence

Debby was in a restaurant with her three-month-old baby, Emma, when someone at the next table suddenly dropped an empty glass, which shattered and showered Emma with splinters of glass. A larger piece cut the baby's hand, which began to bleed profusely. In the rush via taxi to the nearest hospital, Debby felt overwhelmed with fear. She began hyperventilating and started to feel light-headed. Debby knew that she needed to remain as calm as possible in order to take good care of Emma, so she began repeating the phrase, "My breath is calm and regular . . . calm and regular . . . calm and regular," and she could feel her breathing and her racing heart slow down. Although she was still scared, she felt more in control.

Emma only needed two stitches. But when they came home from the hospital, Debby kept picturing the accident, only she imagined the very worst scenarios—Emma blinded or scarred for life. Debby soon realized that she was creating extra anxiety for herself and that she needed to take some time to de-stress. While Emma was resting, Debby lay down nearby and visualized her favorite place at the ocean. Afterward Debby felt refreshed and was able to have a more balanced view of the situation.

Image Rehearsal During and After a Stressful Event Exercise

1. Take a few minutes to relax using your favorite relaxation technique.
2. As you feel yourself becoming more relaxed take a few minutes to visualize yourself in the midst of a stressful situation. Using image rehearsal, imagine yourself using any relaxation technique you wish during the period of most intense stress and see yourself able to be more relaxed and in control.
3. Then picture yourself using a relaxation technique after a stressful event, to help you return to a more balanced state of mind and body.
4. Let go of the images. Relax for a few more minutes. Stretch. Open your eyes slowly and go on with your life.

Assignments

1. Do this Image Rehearsal Exercise today for ten to fifteen minutes. As you become familiar with this exercise you will be able to do it much more quickly.

   If you encounter any unexpected stressful situation—no matter how small—use your choice of relaxation techniques during and after the event.
2. Continue to use image rehearsal of anticipated stressful events whenever necessary (see Lesson 11).
3. Continue doing the quick Body Scan and Diaphragmatic Breathing throughout the day.

   Pay attention to your breathing patterns, especially during stressful situations and continue using your triggers to relaxation throughout the day.
4. Review your Less Stress Goals.

Lesson 13: Sensory Awareness

"Calmness of mind does not mean you should stop your activity. Real calmness should be found in activity itself."

—Shunryu Suzuki

When you are operating under high stress, you are frequently too preoccupied with past and future events to savor and enjoy the present. And the preoccupation with the past and future can create stress, particularly if your memories and dreams are of the what-if, if-only, or wouldn't-it-be-awful variety. An important part of a Less Stress life-style is the ability to live fully in the moment and to appreciate the world, using all your senses.

Awareness will be a key word during the next series of lessons. Awareness means paying attention to your mind, your body, and the world in a nonjudgmental way.

Sensory Awareness Exercise

1. Take a few minutes to relax using your favorite relaxation technique.
2. With your eyes closed, be receptive to your surroundings.
   - What do you hear? Are the sounds loud, soft, piercing, soothing, high-pitched, intermittent, steady? Listen to the sounds.

- What do you smell? Food, flowers, fresh air, stale air, exhaust fumes, wood smoke?
- Rub your hands along nearby surfaces. What do you feel? Notice textures and shapes, hardness, softness, warmth, coldness. Experience how things feel.

3. Open your eyes. Slowly look around you.
   - What do you see? Notice colors, contours, areas of light and dark. Don't comment to yourself on what you see; simply look at your surroundings.

Assignments

1. Take ten to fifteen minutes to do today's Sensory Awareness Exercise.
   Several times today, stop for a few minutes and, using all your senses, pay attention to your surroundings.
2. Continue using image rehearsal and your triggers to relaxation to help you practice your choice of relaxation techniques throughout the day. Remember to relax before, during, and/or after a stressful event.
   Continue to use the quick Body Scan and Diaphragmatic Breathing throughout the day.
3. Review your Less Stress Goals.

Lesson 14: Sensuality Awareness

"There's not a minute of our lives should stretch without some pleasure."

—*Shakespeare,* Antony and Cleopatra

Although our society is far from puritanical, many of you have been taught that it is self-indulgent to be sensual. You touch your body in the bath or shower, but you hardly allow yourself to enjoy the sensations of touch. When was the last time you spent more than a few seconds touching a velvety piece of clothing, giving yourself a face massage, touching another person nonsexually?

Many people consider sexuality to be primarily a genital experience, but your entire body surface can become relaxed and sensualized. Remember that your skin is an erogenous zone—it just needs some attention.

Lavish this kind of love on yourself often. It's relaxing. It feels good.

Sensuality Awareness Exercise

1. Run a warm bath or take a shower at a time when you aren't in a rush. (This can be done alone or as a couple).
   Spend some time in the water with your eyes closed.
   Experience the sensations:
   - wetness
   - warmth
   - tingling.

2. As you soap your body, do it as if you were washing a lover—slow, delicious strokes—kneading, shaking, and caressing your entire body.

   Take time to enjoy the sensations: your soapy skin, the pressure of your hands.

   Wash and massage every part of your body in this luxurious manner.
3. When you finish bathing, pay the same careful attention to the process of drying your body. Tenderly and firmly massage and caress your skin with your towel.

   Rub on some moisturizing lotion with long, soothing strokes all over your body.

   As you get dressed, be aware of the sensations of the fabrics as they touch your skin.
4. Notice how aware you are of your body, how sensual you feel.

Assignments

1. Practice the Sensual Awareness Exercise once today for ten to twenty minutes.

   Sometime during the day give some part of your body a massage. Neck, face, hands, or feet are good places to work on.
2. Continue using image rehearsal and your triggers to relaxation to help you practice your choice of relaxation techniques throughout the day.

   Continue to use the quick Body Scan and Diaphragmatic Breathing throughout the day.
3. Review your Less Stress Goals.

Lesson 15: Eating Awareness

"We live too fast and coarsely, just as we eat too fast. We do not know the true savor of our food."
—Henry David Thoreau

You spend a great deal of time preparing and consuming food, yet often you pay very little attention to the actual experience of eating. You may even bolt your food, barely tasting it. This "fast-food" mentality can cause you to overeat because you don't notice when your body tells you to stop.

Eating, itself, can become a stressful activity.

- You might regularly gain and lose weight.
- You might think of yourself as heavy even if you're at normal weight.
- You might get caught in a cycle of craving certain foods, eating a lot, and feeling guilty.

Some people use eating as a way of escaping from stressful situations; for example, eating a box of chocolate-chip cookies to "treat" themselves after a hard day. Unfortunately erratic eating patterns increase stress on the body.

You can also get a great deal of pleasure from food. As a way of gaining more insight into your relationship to food, as well as learning to more fully enjoy eating, try the following exercise.

Eating Awareness Exercise

1. Choose any natural food, such as fruit, raisins, or nuts.
   Take a small amount of this food in one hand.
   Look at, feel, and smell the food.
   Close your eyes and begin to lift your hand with one piece of food up to your mouth.
2. Place the food in your mouth but don't chew. Just feel its texture, flavor, and temperature.
   Chew once and let the flavor explode on your tongue. Take some time to experience the taste fully.
   Continue chewing. Observe the changing flavors and textures.
   Decide when to swallow and then do so.
3. Notice the aftertaste.
   Notice your thoughts, judgments, or desire for more food.
4. Repeat the exercise. Continue until your body tells you that you have eaten enough.
   Stop eating at this point. What are your thoughts and feelings now?
   - Are you full? Still hungry?
   - What tastes linger?

Assignments

1. Do this Eating Awareness Exercise once today in silence.
   Observe your normal eating habits at all of your meals today. Ask yourself what you have learned about eating and your relationship to food.
   - Did you eat more or less than usual?

- Enjoy food more?
- Were you relaxed or tense during meals?
- Did you eat only when you were hungry? As a response to stress?

2. Continue using image rehearsal and your triggers to relaxation to help you practice your choice of relaxation techniques throughout the day.

   Continue doing the quick Body Scan and Diaphragmatic Breathing throughout the day.
3. Review your Less Stress Goals.

Lesson 16: Awareness of Walking

"Learning to respond to now is all there is to learn."
—Hugh Prather

If you have ever watched a baby taking its first steps, you probably felt amazement that such a tiny creature could master such a complex procedure. Very few of us, unless we've had an accident or illness as an adult, have any memories of our own process of learning how to walk. In fact, those of us who are able to walk easily usually take our ability to walk for granted. Most people merely use walking as a convenient way to get from one place to another, and they are often in such a rush that they are barely aware of the process of walking itself.

Since many of you do spend part of each day walking from place to place, we want you to learn to bring awareness to the act of walking—your movements, the sensations you feel, the sights you see—as a relaxation technique in itself. Learning to slow down just enough to enjoy the process of going from place to place is as important as reaching the goal of "getting somewhere."

If you use a wheelchair to get around, you can do this exercise by paying attention to the movements you make as you navigate your chair.

Awareness of Walking Exercise

1. In your home or outdoors, find a place where you can walk five to ten steps forward without obstruction.
2. Begin to walk very slowly, almost as if you were walking through a roomful of honey. Feel each movement you make—all the muscles that make it possible for you to walk. Notice:
   - shifting your weight
   - lifting your foot
   - placing it down
   - shifting your weight again
   - the sensations in your hips, legs, and feet
   - your breathing.

   Slowly turn around, staying aware of your movements. Walk slowly back to the starting point.
3. If you are in a safe place, close your eyes and repeat this process.

   Now open your eyes and repeat it again, this time paying attention to what you see.

   Whenever your mind wanders during this exercise, bring it back to the present moment by noticing the sensations you feel, the sights you see.

Assignments

1. Do the Awareness of Walking Exercise once today for five or ten minutes.
2. Pay attention to your walking throughout the day. Are you:
   - always in a rush
   - impatient and fidgety when you are waiting in line?

   If you slow down enough to be aware of your movement, do you feel:
   - more relaxation

- less muscular tension
- more enjoyment of walking?

Use this same level of awareness whenever you are going from place to place, even if you are exercising or moving at a quicker pace. While you are driving, bicycling, or jogging, pay attention to your movements, sensations, breathing, and environment. Keep bringing your mind back into the actual experience of the moment.

3. Continue using image rehearsal and your triggers to relaxation to help you practice your choice of relaxation techniques throughout the day.

   Continue to use the quick Body Scan and Diaphragmatic Breathing throughout the day.

4. Review your Less Stress goals.

Lesson 17: Pleasant Moments

"Most men pursue pleasure with such breathless haste that they hurry past it."

—Kierkegaard

It's all too easy to focus on what's wrong with your life —and increase your stress in the process. The mind is continually desiring something new, something better. We call this the *if-only syndrome*:

- If only I had a newer car, then I'd be happy.
- If only I had a better relationship than this one, then I'd be happy.
- If only I were better-looking, then I'd be happy.

One way to reduce stress is to notice and appreciate the positive experiences in your life. This does not mean that you should face unacceptable situations in your life with passivity; however, even in the midst of a great deal of daily stress, it is possible to find things that bring you laughter and joy. Today you will focus on what's right in your life.

Pleasant Moments Exercise

1. Lie down or sit comfortably. Close your eyes if you wish.

Take a few minutes to relax using your favorite relaxation technique.

2. In your mind's eye, review the pleasant moments you've had in the past day or two. These may be very brief, small events, such as stroking a cat, seeing a newborn baby, or peeling and eating a juicy orange.

   Pay attention to the thoughts, feelings, and bodily sensations that accompany your memories. Do you feel:
   - more relaxed
   - more energized
   - happier?
3. Continue relaxing for a few more minutes. When you feel ready, stretch and open your eyes (if they were closed).

   Don't worry if you didn't notice many pleasant events. As you continue with the Less Stress Program you can try to become increasingly aware of the pleasant moments in your day.

Assignments

1. Do the Pleasant Moments Exercise once today.

   Stay aware of pleasant moments and events all day long. Jot them down if you wish. At the end of the day reflect back on the pleasant moments you encountered, and then ask yourself the following questions:
   - Were you aware of the pleasant moments as they occurred or only after they were over?
   - Was it difficult to find pleasant events?
   - Are there pleasant experiences that are no longer in your life? If so, why? Can you bring them back?
   - What patterns, if any, did you notice? Were your pleasant events solitary, sense pleasures, or did they involve other people?

   Did this exercise change your day? If so, how? Were you:

- more relaxed
- aware of what's around you
- able to enjoy small things?

2. Continue using image rehearsal and your triggers to relaxation to help you practice your choice of relaxation techniques throughout the day.

   Continue to use the quick Body Scan and Diaphragmatic Breathing throughout the day.
3. Review your Less Stress Goals.

Lesson 18: Living in the Present—Appreciation

"We can only be said to be alive in those moments when our hearts are conscious of our treasures."
—Thornton Wilder

In Lesson 17 you spent at least one day paying attention to pleasant events. Today we want you to take that lesson a bit further, by learning to pay attention to all aspects of your life—with equal interest and appreciation.

When you look back without bitterness on painful situations in your past, you often discover that you have grown psychologically and/or spiritually from those experiences. For example, Darryl Stingley was a wide receiver for the New England Patriots when he was struck and paralyzed as he dived for a ball. Four years later, he said:

> "For the first time in my life I had encountered something beyond my control. I lost just about everything I had except my life. Then, all of a sudden, it becomes a new way of life. It's redefining who I am now. Everything that was, was. It can no longer be. When you stop asking yourself why, you start living. Now I have a lot of time to sit and think. I started seeing more in a flower—in the lifetime of a flower, in a life itself. It seems to me that a flower understands what its life is like. When it's blooming, its petals are open and full of life. People sometimes don't look at life like that. Now my existence may be shorter. Now I have to try to live more abundantly."

Unfortunately, when you are right in the midst of a difficult situation, you often get lost in your own misery and forget that you could be using the situation to learn more about yourself. By bringing awareness into all your experiences, no matter how painful, you can lose some of your fear. You can begin to trust that you will be able to handle even the greatest losses—the deaths of loved ones and your own death. By "handling" your losses in life, we mean that you can learn how to openly express and feel your sadness without being consumed by bitterness.

Here is another true story that illustrates this point:

> Someone once asked a wise teacher the following question: "How can we be happy when the world is so full of death and loss?" The teacher held up a beautiful and very valuable crystal glass he had been given as a gift. Pointing to the glass, he said, "When I look through this glass, I love to see the sunlight turn into a prism of colors. It is so beautiful. When I hold the glass, I enjoy running my fingers across its smooth, delicate surface. And how I love to drink from it. Such a precious object, yet I already imagine it lying broken in a thousand pieces. So when, someday, inevitably, a child comes and knocks over this glass . . . ah, so it has already been broken. And in just this way I try to see all of my relationships as finite. Therefore, each time I am with a loved one, it is precious. I am grateful for each moment we spend together and less fearful of the separation to come."

The acceptance of the impermanence of life is one of our greatest challenges and the most basic key to deep inner relaxation. Today's exercise may help you begin to appreciate more fully the preciousness of each moment of your life.

Living in the Present Exercise

1. Lie down or sit comfortably. Close your eyes.
   Take a few minutes to relax using your favorite relaxation technique.
2. Now begin to focus your attention on your breathing. Begin to imagine that each breath you take is your last breath. What feelings do you have?
   - sadness
   - fear
   - regrets of things undone, words unspoken
   - peace?
3. Picture some of the important people in your life. Imagine yourself openly expressing appreciation and showing affection to them. Remember some of the kind things they have done for you.
4. Now *you* are the important person. Picture yourself and begin to tell yourself silently what you appreciate about yourself, such as:
   - your feet, for taking you around each day
   - your entire body
   - your ability to laugh and cry
   - your ability to see, hear, move, and talk
   - your ability to think and to feel
   - your ability to contemplate the mystery of life and death.
5. Return to the awareness of your breathing. Notice how remarkable the breath, itself, is. It is your link to life. Appreciate your ability to breathe automatically, all day and night.
   Stretch and appreciate your muscles for being able to move. Even if they feel tense or weak, pay attention to each movement you make, as if it is your last.
   Open your eyes and appreciate what you see around you, even if it is just the same old apartment. Notice the colors, shapes, textures. How fortunate it is to be able

to see. Imagine that this is the last time you will be able to see anything.

6. Continue with your day, imagining that this is your last day on earth.

Assignments

1. Do the Living in the Present Exercise today. All day, imagine that this is your last day and see how the awareness affects your ability to pay attention to all aspects of your life:
   - your senses
   - your communications
   - your thoughts and feelings
   - your activities.

   Every morning, for the rest of these lessons (for the rest of your life, if you wish), begin the day with a few minutes of appreciation—for your body, your mind, your loved ones, the world around you.
2. Continue using image rehearsal and your triggers to relaxation to help you practice your choice of relaxation techniques throughout the day.

   Continue using the quick Body Scan and Diaphragmatic Breathing throughout the day.
3. Review your Less Stress Goals.

Lesson 19: Awareness of Mind Chatter

"The mind is its own place and in itself can make a heaven of hell, a hell of heaven."

—*John Milton*

Many people think that events directly cause emotions.

Linda J., 29, single, clerk in a bookstore

Linda was going out on a blind date one night. Talking to a friend at work before she went out on the date, she said, "I hate blind dates. They make me so scared, I get sick to my stomach."

However, there's an important step between an event and your emotional response to it. We, along with many stress counselors, call this step *mind chatter*. Everyone has an internal monologue, a running commentary on the world around them. Sometimes this can be High Stress mind chatter. Linda, anticipating her blind date, might have said to herself:

- "I'm too fat."
- "What if I'm boring?"

- "He won't have anything to say."
- "I'll say something stupid."
- "I'll fall in love, but he'll never call back."
- "Maybe he's shorter than I am. How awful."

And on and on. These thoughts, rather than the blind date itself, caused Linda's feelings of stress. Today's exercise will help you tune into your own mind chatter and begin to learn how thoughts can influence your response to stress.

Mind Chatter Exercise

1. Lie down or sit comfortably. Close your eyes if you wish, and scan your body for tension.

   As you practice diaphragmatic breathing let your tension drain away.

   Tighten and relax any unusually tense areas.
2. When you feel relaxed, begin to visualize a recent stressful event—nothing major, maybe an incident at work or a fight with your kids or a near-miss traffic accident.

   Replay the incident in detail. Note the changes in your body, such as tightening of muscles, rapid heartbeat, tight breathing, "butterflies" in your stomach.

   Replay the scene again, paying attention to your mind chatter as the stressor occurs.
   - What does your inner voice sound like? Is it angry? exasperated? tolerant? sad? judgmental?
   - What are you saying?
   - Are they soothing, nurturing phrases? Or negative, judgmental phrases?

   Listen to your mind chatter.
3. Return to diaphragmatic breathing for a few minutes and let yourself relax again. When you are ready, take some deeper breaths, stretch, and slowly open your eyes.

Write down, in the spaces below, your stressor and the accompanying mind chatter.

Your Stressor

____

____

____

Your Mind Chatter

____

____

____

Assignments

1. Do this Awareness of Mind Chatter Exercise once today.
2. Throughout the day, when you react to a stressor, stop and recall the thoughts that immediately preceded your reaction.
3. Start each day with some moments of appreciation.

   Continue using image rehearsal and your triggers to relaxation to help you practice your choice of relaxation techniques throughout the day.

   Continue to use the quick Body Scan and Diaphragmatic Breathing throughout the day.
4. Review your Less Stress Goals.

Lesson 20: Beliefs

"Change your thoughts and you change your world."
—Norman Vincent Peale

The last lesson helped you tune into High Stress mind chatter. This mind chatter frequently is based on—and reinforces—beliefs you have about the world: who you are, who you should be, what you expect, what you deserve.

For example, Linda J.'s fearful mind chatter (see pp. 97–98) was based primarily on the High Stress beliefs that:

- I should never look foolish.
- I should have complete control over events in my life.
- I should be perfect.

Beliefs Exercise

1. Take a few minutes to relax using your favorite relaxation technique.
2. When you are relaxed, open your eyes and return to yesterday's lesson. Review the stressor and the mind chatter you wrote down.
3. Without censoring yourself, write down some of the deeply held beliefs your mind chatter reflects.

Your Belief List

1. ______________________________
2. ______________________________
3. ______________________________

Assignments

1. Take ten to fifteen minutes to relax and complete today's Beliefs Exercise.
   Look at your list throughout the day and think about these beliefs. Where did they come from? Do they help you? Do they get in your way?
2. Start each day with some moments of appreciation. Continue using image rehearsal and your triggers to relaxation to help you practice your choice of relaxation techniques throughout the day.
   Continue to use the quick Body Scan and Diaphragmatic Breathing throughout the day.
3. Review your Less Stress Goals.

Lesson 21: Challenging and Changing Your Beliefs

"We've been 'should on' all of our lives. It's time to let go of 'Should's.' "

—Stephen Levine

Many of your beliefs help you cope positively with your life, but some of them only increase stress. Beliefs that are stated as absolutes, either/or choices, "should's," "ought's," or "must's" frequently increase your stress.

Challenging and restating High Stress Beliefs so that they become Less Stress Beliefs is an important stress-management technique to learn.

A Less Stress way to state Linda J.'s beliefs (see p. 100) is:

- It is okay to look foolish sometimes.
- I can't control everything in my life. I am a good person even if bad things happen to me.
- Other people's values and evaluations are important, but they don't run my life. I can respect myself if I behave in a way consistent with my values.

Challenging and Changing Your Beliefs Exercise

1. Take a few minutes to relax using your favorite relaxation technique.

   Open your eyes. Review yesterday's list of beliefs.
2. For each High Stress Belief answer these questions:
   - How does this belief contribute to my stress?
   - Is this a logical belief?
   - Is this a realistic belief? Can I expect myself, or anyone else, to live up to this belief?
   - Who taught me this belief? Does it suit my life now?

   For each High Stress Belief restate the belief so it is more balanced, realistic, more suited to a Less Stress life-style.

Your Less Stress Belief List

1. ______________________________

   ____
2. ______________________________

   ____
3. ______________________________

   ____

Assignments

1. Take ten to fifteen minutes to relax and complete today's Challenging and Changing Beliefs Exercise. Practice your new beliefs by repeating them to yourself throughout the day. *Remember*—you've held the old beliefs for a long time. This week is just the beginning of

a new way of looking at things. Challenging the old beliefs and accepting the new ones will take practice.

2. Start each day with some moments of appreciation.

   Continue using image rehearsal and your triggers to relaxation to help you practice your choice of relaxation techniques throughout the day.

   Continue using the quick Body Scan and Diaphragmatic Breathing throughout the day.

3. Review your Less Stress Goals.

Lesson 22: Less Stress Mind Chatter

"People who feel good about themselves produce good results."

—Kenneth Blanchard

Although it takes time to change your beliefs, you can experience immediate Less Stress benefits by tuning into and changing your High Stress mind chatter into Less Stress mind chatter.

For example, before Linda's (see p. 102) next blind date, she might say to herself:

- I'm a good person even if this particular man doesn't ask me out again.
- I'm intelligent. I don't always have to be brilliant and witty.
- He might be nervous, too.

Less Stress Mind Chatter Exercise

1. Return to Lesson 19 and review your stressor and mind chatter.
2. Take a few minutes to relax using your favorite relaxation technique.
3. Visualize the scene again.

Substitute Less Stress mind chatter.
How do you feel?
Record your Less Stress mind chatter below.

Less Stress Mind Chatter

1. ______________________________

____

2. ______________________________

____

3. ______________________________

____

Assignments

1. Take ten to fifteen minutes to relax and complete today's Less Stress Mind Chatter Exercise.
   As stressful events occur throughout your day practice substituting Less Stress mind chatter.
2. Start each day with some moments of appreciation.
   Continue using image rehearsal and your triggers to relaxation to help you practice your choice of relaxation techniques throughout the day.
   Continue to use the quick Body Scan and Diaphragmatic Breathing throughout the day.
3. Review your Less Stress Goals.

Lesson 23: Active Listening Awareness

"Do not permit the events of your daily lives to bind you, but never withdraw yourselves from them."

—Huang-Po

You spend a great deal of your life hearing other people talk, but often you aren't really listening at all. Instead, you are busy formulating your own responses before the other person finishes speaking—or you simply may be drifting in daydreams.

An argument is usually created by two people who won't listen—two people who each care more about being right than about hearing and empathizing with the other person's point of view. You can improve your ability to communicate if you slow down your conversations enough so you don't automatically interrupt the other person.

Most people want, above all, to feel heard and understood. It is not necessary to agree with another person, but it is also not necessary to fight just because there are two different points of view.

Steve and Louise E., 56 and 53, married couple

Steve and Louise argue frequently about Louise's daughter, Maggie, who is twenty-four and lives away from home. Here is a typical argument:

Louise: I'm feeling real guilty about not sending Maggie any extra money this month.

Steve: It's not your fault that she squanders every penny you—

Louise *(interrupting; her voice gets louder):* She does not squander her money. Things are just real expensive where she lives and she's just learning how to balance—

Steve *(sarcastically):* Maggie couldn't balance a budget if she tried. She's addicted to shopping, and she's always buying clothes like they're going out of style. She just doesn't deserve anything more from you until she learns to give something back. You paid her college expenses and she never so much as sends you a damn birthday card.

Louise: You don't understand me at all. I don't expect anything back from her. She's only a kid and I'm sure—

Steve: I'm sure she'll never grow up if you keep rescuing her.

Louise *(screaming as she walks out of the room):* You have no heart, you jerk.

As you can see, Louise wanted her feelings to be heard. When Steve immediately attacked her without listening, she got angry and was unable to listen to Steve's advice, even if what he was trying to say included some important truths. Both Steve and Louise wound up feeling agitated, angry, and not cared about.

Here is the same discussion handled more skillfully, by using active listening techniques.

Louise: I'm feeling really guilty about not sending Maggie any extra money this month.

Steve: What's making you feel so guilty?

Louise: I'm just not sure how to handle this situation. Maggie has barely saved enough to pay her rent—she called up crying again this morning—but she still owes me money from the last loan. I feel so stingy, though. She's only twenty-four, and I know it's tough out there. Everything costs so much more than it did when we were kids.

Steve: It sounds like you're feeling real confused again about how to deal with Maggie. Do you want to talk some more about your thoughts and feelings?

Louise: Well, it feels great to be heard rather than contradicted, even if my feelings are irrational. Do you have any advice?

Steve: Are you sure you feel ready to hear my opinion now?

Louise: Yes, thanks.

The following Active Listening Exercise can help you practice being a good listener. Learning to be attentive to others can help your productivity at work—and can help you avoid unnecessary arguments at home. After all, the word *communicate* really means "to be in communion."

Active Listening Exercise

1. Take a few minutes to do your favorite relaxation technique. When your mind and body feel more relaxed, picture the last argument you had—at work or at home. If you can't remember a recent argument, picture a person who often annoys or angers you and imagine an argument you might have with this person.
2. Now picture yourself having the same discussion but using active listening techniques:
   - Pay careful attention to the other person.
   - Restrain yourself from interrupting.
   - Don't jump to your own defense even if the other person criticizes you.
   - When the other person has finished, verbally paraphrase what they said.
   - Ask the other person if they feel understood.
   - Continue to listen and paraphrase until the other person feels understood.
   - Ask the person if you can respond after they feel heard and understood. Try to respond without defensiveness. Speak slowly as you tell the other per-

son how you felt after listening to their opinions or criticisms. Remember, it's possible to express anger without screaming and yelling.

3. Return for a few minutes to your favorite relaxation technique. When you feel ready, stretch and go on with the day.

Assignments

1. Do the Active Listening Exercise once today.

   If you have a difficult conversation or argument today, try to practice active listening. If not, remember to use this technique the next time you are in conflict with another person.
2. Start each day with some moments of appreciation. Continue using image rehearsal and your triggers to relaxation to help you practice your choice of relaxation techniques throughout the day.

   Continue to use the quick Body Scan and Diaphragmatic Breathing throughout the day.
3. Review your Less Stress Goals.

Lesson 24: Expressing Anger Skillfully

"Life is a series of problems. Do we want to moan about them or solve them?"

—Scott Peck, M.D.

Most people assume that it is necessary to give up being angry in order to become a deeply relaxed individual. While it is true that anger often comes from a habitual reaction to certain types of people and events, it is a natural emotion. Even the smallest baby gets angry when she doesn't get her way. As children we scream, cry, or pout to express our anger and disappointment, but as adults we can learn more skillful ways of expressing our anger. Here is an example of a typical situation.

Donald G., 42, married, father of three, lawyer

Donald was recently made a senior partner in a small law firm, and the competition in his part of the country is fierce. All of his partners have to work overtime just to keep the firm solvent. Lately, Donald has been waking up in the early-morning hours, drenched in sweat, with horrible nightmares—most of them involving financial collapse and courtroom fiascoes. He is exhausted much of the time and very irritable with his wife, Melissa, and the children. One evening Melissa and the kids went to an awards ceremony at the grade school. When they arrived home, Donald was deeply involved in reading his law journals and was in no mood to be disturbed. His nine-year-old daughter, Meaghan, came over to show him the book she had won as a prize for an essay, and Donald looked up impatiently and snapped at her, saying, "I'm busy, I'll look at it tomorrow." Then Melissa yelled at Donald for not being supportive to the children, and the evening ended in a way that has become more and more familiar in their household—everyone stalked off to their rooms feeling sad and angry. Donald worked alone in his study until 1 A.M. After trying to quiet his whirling mind he finally fell asleep on the couch at 2:30 A.M.

In many cases people direct their anger at inappropriate targets; in Donald's case, he yelled at his small daughter. On the surface it seemed that Donald was mad at Meaghan for disturbing him, but underlying this superficial layer of anger was a much deeper issue: Donald's fear of failure at work. By carefully observing your thoughts when you feel angry, you can become aware of your underlying feelings. As you learn to clarify the root causes of your anger, you can learn how to express your anger more effectively and appropriately.

Some Typical Ways of Expressing Anger

1. Blaming and attacking statements	"It's all your fault that . . ."
2. Sarcastic statements	"You *sure* did a *great* job on that . . ."
3. Aggressive yelling and screaming at another person; abusive language	"You stupid son-of-a-bitch."

4. Pouting and/or withdrawal	"Nothing's wrong."
5. Guilt-inducing statements	"I knew you wouldn't do enough . . ."
6. Throwing and breaking household objects	

WARNING: Anger that leads to violence toward other people is *never* appropriate. If you are unable to control your anger to this degree, please seek professional help.

More Skillful Ways of Expressing Anger

1. "I" statements expressing your own feelings	"I feel angry when you do . . ."
2. Discovering the underlying feelings and revealing them openly	"I'm upset and angry about my work situation and I feel too impatient to look at your book tonight, Meaghan. I will look at it when I feel better."

3. Expressing the little moments of anger as they arise, rather than letting them build to an explosive level

4. It may be helpful to yell, scream, or punch—but not directed at another person. You can go into an empty room or sit in a parked car, roll up the windows, and scream at the top of your lungs or recite an angry tirade. Or hit a thick foam pillow or mattress. It's healthy to let off steam and to release your angry feelings, but you don't need to dump your rage directly on another individual. After releasing some of your surface anger you

can approach the person more rationally and calmly to discuss the issue.

5. You could try writing in a journal or writing an angry letter to the other person (without sending it) to let off steam or to gain some perspective on the issue. Try writing a dialogue between you and the other person to help you see their point of view with less defensiveness.

6. For more ways to deal skillfully with your anger see the listings under "Psychology and Meditation" in Suggested Reading (p. 146).

Changing your patterns of expressing anger may take quite a long time and some hard work and the process involves continual awareness. Paying attention to your actions and the results of those actions is the best way to learn.

Expressing Anger Skillfully Exercise

1. Lie down or sit comfortably. Close your eyes if you wish.

   Take a few minutes to relax using your favorite relaxation technique.
2. Remember and visualize the last time you were angry. What did you think, say, feel, and do? If you feel dissatisfied with your approach, picture yourself handling the situation in new, more skillful ways. See yourself using awareness to help you uncover the root causes of your anger and to help you remember that you have a choice of ways in which to deal with that anger.
3. Let go of the images and relax again for a few minutes. When you are ready, stretch and open your eyes (if they were closed).

Assignments

1. Do this Expressing Anger Skillfully Exercise once today.

   During the day notice small and larger moments or situations involving anger (your own or other people's). What is the underlying cause of the anger? Be very observant of the entire interaction. Try to notice what ways of expressing anger you usually use. If you feel angry, try using a relaxation technique right then to calm your mind in order to make a more skillful choice. These patterns are usually difficult to change, so be patient and keep working on this exercise from now on.
2. Start each day with some moments of appreciation.

   Continue using image rehearsal and your triggers to relaxation to help you practice your choice of relaxation techniques throughout the day.

   Continue using the quick Body Scan and Diaphragmatic Breathing throughout the day.
3. Review your Less Stress Goals.

Lesson 25: Assertiveness Skills I

"Even when you're on the right track, you'll get run over if you just sit there."

—Old proverb

JoAnn H., 31, divorced mother of two, bookkeeper

JoAnn has always had difficulty expressing anger and usually backs off from conflict. She got divorced three years ago and shares custody of her two children with her ex-husband. Most of the time things go smoothly—there's nothing bad about the way Mike deals with the kids, it's just different from her way; but JoAnn dreads Mondays when the kids come back from Mike's house. They seem pretty confused sometimes, and hard to handle. Her big concern right now is the amount of TV they watch at Mike's. Last week seven-year-old Carla started whining and crying when JoAnn made her turn off the TV and go to bed at 9:00 P.M. JoAnn wants to ask Mike to limit the TV time, but she's afraid to talk to him. Discussions with Mike rarely go well. She either yells or pleads—nothing in between. And, as Mike says, what right does she have to interfere with him and the kids?

JoAnn doesn't know how to be assertive with Mike, and that has become a major source of stress for her. When she tries to stand up for herself, she usually goes too far and starts accusing and attacking; the discussion turns into a blazing fight. JoAnn makes the common mistake of confusing assertive behavior with aggressive behavior.

Assertive behavior respects both you and the other person. As an assertive person, you know what's important to you, you make choices about your behavior based on that knowledge, but you don't push your values onto other people. You communicate clearly, directly, and specifically, using objective words and "I" messages, in a relaxed, open manner with direct eye contact. For example, "I am concerned about the amount of TV the kids watch at your house" is an assertive statement.

Aggressive behavior expresses your rights but violates the other person's rights and feelings. When you are aggressive, you blame the other person. You speak in a tense or patronizing manner, perhaps using a loud, disapproving voice. Instead of citing facts, you confuse feelings with fact. "You're an incompetent, thoughtless parent to let the kids watch all that junk on TV" is an aggressive statement.

Passive behavior denies your rights. When you are passive, you use apologetic words and a weak, hesitant voice. You hedge and qualify statements. You might say assertive words, but you will say them with a teary-eyed, pleading look. "Do you think maybe sometimes you could monitor the kids' TV watching? No big deal, but you know . . ." is a passive statement.

As you read these definitions, think about your own behavior. Which category do you fit into most often? Many people are able to be assertive in some situations and not in others. You might find it easy to act assertively with a friend but not with your garage mechanic or boss. You may fight fair with a colleague and bully your spouse. You might find that your greatest difficulty is saying no to someone who asks for a favor, or setting limits, or dividing up work fairly.

Understanding what assertive behavior is and recognizing your patterns are important steps toward becoming more assertive. Also, being assertive increases self-esteem, which is a key to deep inner relaxation. In the next three exercises, you will be working on developing your assertiveness skills.

Assertiveness Skills Exercise

1. Take a few minutes to relax using your favorite relaxation technique.
2. Review the past week. Think about a few times when you needed to speak up for yourself—with your boss, your spouse, your kids, your parents, a salesperson. Calmly review the scenes that come to you:
   - Does one time stand out?
   - What happened?
   - Who were you talking to?
   - What about?
   - How did you behave?
   - What did you say?
   - How did they respond?
   - What was the outcome?
   - How did you feel during the conversation?
   - How did you feel after the conversation?
3. Let go of the images and relax again for a few minutes. When you are ready, stretch, and open your eyes.

Assignments

1. Do the Assertiveness Skills Exercise at least once today.

   Be aware of your behavior during the day today. Observe yourself with a noncritical eye. When are you assertive? passive? aggressive?
2. Start each day with some moments of appreciation.

   Continue using image rehearsal and your triggers to relaxation to help you practice your choice of relaxation techniques throughout the day.

   Continue to use the quick Body Scan and Diaphragmatic Breathing throughout the day.
3. Review your Less Stress Goals.

Lesson 26: Assertiveness II—What Are Your Rights?

"What would life be if we had no courage to attempt anything?"

—*Van Gogh*

JoAnn (see p. 116) often worries about her rights regarding the kids and her negotiations with Mike. On the one hand, JoAnn grew up believing she should be selfless and nurturing to everyone, that her opinions were always open to question, that she should always be agreeable, and that she should never make mistakes. On the other hand, as the children's mother, she does have some fairly strong opinions about what's best for them, and she believes it's her responsibility to give them the best possible life.

It's easy enough to read about assertiveness skills. "Seems pretty straightforward," you might say, "but really, what right do I have to . . . ?" That question, "What right do I have?" is one of the biggest stumbling blocks to assertive behavior. Many of you learned at an early age that it wasn't okay to believe in yourself and stand up for your rights. You might believe that you should be perfect, selfless, always logical, always flexible, always responsive to others, etc. Changing beliefs about who you are and what you deserve can take time, practice, and, perhaps, the help of other people. The Less Stress Lessons can help you begin the process of change.

Here's the beginning of a list of assertive rights compiled by many experts in the assertiveness field. How do these rights sound to you?

"I have a right to:

- say no without guilt
- express my feelings and opinions
- ask for help
- change my mind
- make mistakes
- be treated respectfully
- choose not to respond
- put myself first sometimes
- be alone
- choose not to be assertive."

Assertiveness II Exercise

1. Take a few minutes to relax using the relaxation method of your choice.
2. When you are ready, look at the list of rights given above. Read it through a few times.
   - Which rights do you agree with?
   - Which rights do you disagree with?
   - Why do you disagree?
   - What would you change or add?

   Make your own list of assertive rights or expand this list.
3. Keep the list to review and change periodically.

Assignments

1. Do the Assertiveness II Exercise once today.
2. Start each day with some moments of appreciation. Continue using image rehearsal and your triggers to re-

laxation to help you practice your choice of relaxation techniques throughout the day.

Continue to use the quick Body Scan and Diaphragmatic Breathing throughout the day.

3. Review your Less Stress goals.

Lesson 27: Assertiveness III—Techniques

"If you have something difficult to do, don't expect people to roll stones out of your way."

—*Albert Schweitzer*

Now that you've spent some time reviewing your own behavior patterns and thinking about your rights to assertive behavior, and it's time to learn some specific techniques.

When you need to be assertive in a specific situation, many assertiveness experts recommend the following steps:

1. *Identify the goal for each encounter.* What bothers you? What do you want to change? Try to focus clearly and specifically on just one goal.
2. *Ask yourself some questions.* What are your rights? What are the risks? What are the benefits?
3. *Don't wait.* Timing is crucial. The faster you can respond assertively to a disturbing event, the more effective you will be.
4. *Rehearse.* Use Image Rehearsal techniques to imagine yourself acting assertively, aggressively, passively. How do you feel in each instance? Do you feel powerful, nervous, confident, relaxed, angry? Write out an assertive script for yourself. Practice with a friend or your mirror or a tape recorder.

5. *Make honest, direct statements.* Speak for yourself using "I" messages. Don't blame or accuse.
6. *Describe behavior objectively.* Don't evaluate or judge. For example, "You didn't clean up the dishes last night" is an objective statement. "You're a lazy slob" is not an objective statement.
7. *Restate the message* until the other person understands you.
8. *Make clear, specific, reasonable requests for change.*
9. *Acknowledge the positive consequences of change.*

Let's take a look at JoAnn's situation.

Goal: JoAnn's goal is to reach an agreement with Mike about what the kids watch on TV.

Rights: As a parent, she has the right to opinions concerning her children's well-being.

She has the right to disagree with Mike.

She has the right to negotiate with Mike for a change in the situation.

She has a right to be heard.

Mike's rights are similar to JoAnn's.

Risks: That the discussion will reach a stalemate or that Mike will be angry.

Benefits: Positive change will occur.

When: When Mike brings the kids home on Monday, JoAnn will ask him if they can get together within the next couple of days to talk. She'll try to find a mutually agreeable time and place.

What she'll say: "When the kids come to me on Monday, we usually end up fighting about when they can watch TV and what they can watch. From what they and you have said it seems that your rules are different from mine. I'm concerned about this—the kids seem confused, and I get angry when they challenge me all the time. I'd like us to come up with a consistent set of rules about TV."

Please remember, learning to be assertive takes time and practice. Start small, practice with friends, read some of the books in Suggested Reading, p. 144, or take a class if one is available in your area.

Also remember, assertiveness is a choice. Don't cause yourself more stress by thinking you always have to be assertive in every situation. And even when you are assertive, you may not be able to change things. Assertiveness is frequently effective, but it is not magic. Acceptance of a situation may be the Less Stress strategy of choice. Choosing acceptance does not necessarily mean you are being passive.

Assertiveness III (Techniques) Exercise

1. Take a few minutes to relax using your favorite relaxation technique.
2. Think about a situation that occurred recently when you could have been assertive but weren't.

   Using your visualization skills, replay the scene as it happened.

   Now picture the scene again, using assertiveness skills. What could you do differently?
3. Let go of that scene. Continue relaxing. When you are ready, turn your attention to a future event in which you would like to be assertive.

   Answer the following questions about your specific situation:
   - What is my goal?
   - What are my rights?
   - What are the other person's rights?
   - What are the risks?
   - What are the possible benefits?

- When and where will I talk with him/her?
- What will I say?

Write the answers down if you wish.

4. Let go of the images and relax again for a few minutes. When you are ready, stretch, and open your eyes.

Assignments

1. Do the Assertiveness Techniques III Exercise once today. Continue to be aware of your behavior throughout the day. Practice acting assertively whenever you can. When is it easy to be assertive? When is it difficult?
2. Start each day with some moments of appreciation.

   Continue using image rehearsal and your triggers to relaxation to help you practice your choice of relaxation techniques throughout the day.

   Continue using the quick Body Scan and Diaphragmatic Breathing throughout the day.
3. Review your Less Stress Goals.

Lesson 28: Letting Go of Anger— Learning to Forgive

"Inner peace can be reached only when we practice forgiveness."

—Gerald Jampolsky, M.D.

One belief that people frequently have is: "If I feel hurt by someone else, it's all their fault. I should be angry at them for a long time, especially if they won't apologize."

Certainly it's true that other people can be insensitive and even quite cruel. Growing up with an abusive or alcoholic parent can teach you this lesson early in life. Unfortunately, if you harbor anger toward other people, even those who hurt you badly in the past, you are only hurting yourself in the present.

With very deep childhood hurts, or after a painful divorce or the suicide of a loved one, it may be necessary to work with a qualified therapist to release the pain and anger before you can be ready to forgive. However, many people carry grudges of much less importance—toward a family member, a neighbor, or a co-worker who was nasty to them years ago. Letting go of anger at such people doesn't mean that you are being passive or condoning their actions. But remember: no matter what they did, it was *your perception* that turned their actions into long-lasting stressors for you.

Helen S., 63, widow, retired bank officer

Helen lost her mother to cancer fifteen years ago. After the funeral, Helen's brother, Craig, moved most of their mother's expensive antiques into his house without even consulting Helen. She confronted him, and he gave Helen half of the furniture, but only after some bitter words were spoken between them. Even though he eventually apologized, Helen has never been able to let go of her anger. When she sees Craig at family gatherings, she remembers, in detail, the nasty scenes after her mother's funeral, and she has never been able to reestablish any of their earlier bonds.

Letting go of anger can be a huge relief—like taking off a gigantic, heavy backpack you've been carrying around for years. You might choose to confront the person openly and tell them about your feelings. However, sometimes this isn't possible—the person may have died or moved far away—and sometimes confrontation just doesn't help. But you can still let go of anger in your own heart.

The following exercise can be quite a powerful experience if you allow yourself to really feel your emotions. It may take many repetitions to get past your anger and to feel forgiveness. As with changing all of your deeply held beliefs, you may need to practice forgiveness before you actually can feel it. You can see for yourself how letting go of old anger can lead to Less Stress by following today's exercise.

Learning to Forgive Exercise

1. You may wish to put on a tape of quiet instrumental music. Lie down and close your eyes.

   Take a few minutes to relax using your favorite relaxation technique.

2. Begin to create a picture in your imagination of a place where you feel safe and comfortable. It might be a room or a place in nature from your past or present life. Or you can create an imaginary place.

   Picture yourself in this secure and peaceful place. Hear the sounds, smell the odors, and see the colors and objects in this place. See yourself relaxing deeply in this place.
3. Imagine that a person who has been the focus of your anger is entering your safe place. You have invited him or her into your world. See this person clearly and allow them to sit down. Look into their eyes. See them as a human being like yourself—a person in pain who suffers just as you do.

   In your imagination tell this person about your feelings—your hurt, your sadness, your anger. Express the emotions you have been carrying around inside you.

   When you feel ready, silently tell this person that you forgive them. Tell them that it is time for you to let go of your anger toward them. Continue to say this to them, even if the words feel unfamiliar and uncomfortable.
4. When you are ready, say good-bye and let this person leave your safe place.

   If you are feeling sad or happy, just allow yourself to rest and experience these emotions for a while.
5. Stretch and slowly open your eyes.

Assignments

1. Practice the Learning to Forgive Exercise once today. If there is no one in your life you need to forgive, congratulate yourself and do any of the previous exercises. You can also use this exercise to be forgiven or to forgive yourself. If you have done or said anything to someone else that you still regret, try imagining the per-

son forgiving you and/or try forgiving yourself.

Throughout the day look for any opportunity to let go of anger and forgive.

2. Start each day with some moments of appreciation.

   Continue using image rehearsal and your triggers to relaxation to help you practice your choice of relaxation techniques throughout the day.

   Continue to use the quick Body Scan and Diaphragmatic Breathing throughout the day.
3. Review your Less Stress Goals.

Lesson 29: Looking Back—Reflections

"Keep a sense of humor about all things and stay simple and easy."

—Joseph Goldstein

It's time to reflect on the discoveries and changes that you've made while practicing the Less Stress Lessons.

Do you remember Sally G.'s stress diary (see p. 31)? Sally had difficulty in concentrating, low back pain, and sexual problems with her husband. Sally worked with the Less Stress Program, and here's a list of some of the changes she's noticed in her life:

1. Most important, I can decrease or increase stress by what I tell myself! I see how I'm a perfectionist and I'm trying to be easier on myself. I know this will take a lot of work to change, but I'm willing to do it.
2. I'm finally learning how to take care of myself and not always putting Hank and the kids first. I'm setting limits —at work and at home.
3. I realized that Hank and I need time together without the kids. We set aside two nights a week just for us. We're learning how to talk to each other again—about

feelings as well as events. I've wanted to make love more often since we've started talking, and I've felt more relaxed.

4. Breath awareness and gentle stretching have mostly replaced the muscle relaxants I was taking. My back is starting to improve.

Reflections Exercise

1. Take a few minutes to relax using your favorite relaxation technique. Close your eyes if you wish.
2. Let your mind wander back over the past twenty-eight lessons and your experiences while practicing the exercises. How did you feel when you started the program? What were your goals? How do you feel now? What have you achieved?

   Continue to relax, letting these images and thoughts float through your mind.
3. Open your eyes slowly. When you are ready, write down some of your discoveries, as Sally did, so you'll have a record of what you've achieved.

Your Less Stress Discoveries

1. ______________________________

   ____

2. ______________________________

   ____

3. ______________________________

   ____

4. ______________________________

   ____

5. ______________________________

____

Assignments

1. Do the Reflections Exercise once today.
   During the day, jot down any other changes you notice in your behavior. Look for even subtle changes in the way you respond to stressful situations.
2. Start each day with some moments of appreciation. Continue using image rehearsal and your triggers to relaxation to help you practice your choice of relaxation techniques throughout the day.
   Continue to use the quick Body Scan and Diaphragmatic Breathing throughout the day.
3. Review your Less Stress Goals.

Lesson 30: Setting Your New Less Stress Goals

"Take a minute. Look at your goals. Look at your performance. See if your behavior matches your goals."
—Kenneth Blanchard

In Lesson 29 you reviewed your progress so far. Hopefully you've learned some better ways to manage your stress, but you can't change everything about your life at once. No doubt there's more work to do. It's time to re-evaluate your initial Less Stress Goals.

- Have you achieved your goals?
- What progress have you made?

If you made no progress on a goal, was your goal too vague or too difficult to accomplish?

While doing the Less Stress exercises you have learned which stressful events tend to push your buttons, and, hopefully, you have gained some control over them. Now it's time to set new goals. Working on making specific changes in your behavior is much more productive than just saying to yourself, "I want to be a more relaxed person." To help you be more specific we want you to write down several action steps under each new goal.

For example, June M. was stuck in a dead-end job. She wanted to use more of her intelligence, but the boss kept giving her routine tasks. After doing the Less Stress Lessons, June learned to relax and felt less caught up in her day-to-day hassles. In this clearer state of mind she was able to reevaluate her skills and her work goals. Two of June's new Less Stress Goals are:

1. I want to find a new job within the next three months.
   Action Steps:
   a. Visit local employment agencies and see what's available. Take one day off work to do this.
   b. Rewrite résumé to emphasize the kind of work skills I want to use in my next job.
   c. Send away for newspapers from several larger cities in the state.
   d. Ask a stylish friend to help me pick out a nice wardrobe for job interviews.
2. I want to practice relaxation techniques on a regular basis so I can use them whenever I need them.
   Action Steps:
   a. I will begin by redoing the exercises in the Less Stress Lessons.
   b. I will take a relaxation break at least once a day at work.
   c. I'm going to cut my sugar intake by half and reduce my caffeine intake to one cup of coffee a day.

Setting Your New Less Stress Goals Exercise

1. Take some time now to relax, reflect and write down your new Less Stress Goals and the Action Steps you will take to make these goals happen. Remember: You are setting new priorities in your life and learning to take control over your habitual stress reactions.

GOAL 1: ______________________________

____

Action Steps:

a. ______________________________

b. ______________________________

c. ______________________________

GOAL 2: ______________________________

____

Action Steps:

a. ______________________________

b. ______________________________

c. ______________________________

GOAL 3: ______________________________

____

Action Steps:

a. ______________________________

b. ______________________________

c. ______________________________

Assignments

1. Do the Setting Your New Less Stress Goals Exercise today.
2. Start every day with some moments of appreciation.

   Continue using image rehearsal and your triggers to relaxation to help you practice your choice of relaxation techniques throughout the day and for the rest of your life.

Continue to use the quick Body Scan and Diaphragmatic Breathing throughout the day and for the rest of your life.

3. Pat yourself on the back for having completed your commitment to yourself by doing all of the Less Stress Lessons!

CONGRATULATE YOURSELF! YOU HAVE FINISHED THE LESS STRESS LESSONS. YOU ARE LEARNING TO BE MORE AWARE OF YOUR PATTERNS OF STRESS REACTIONS. YOU ARE NO LONGER AT THE MERCY OF THE OLD, CONDITIONED TAPES IN YOUR MIND—NO LONGER A PRISONER OF HIGH STRESS BELIEFS AND MIND CHATTER. AS YOU CONTINUE PRACTICING LESS STRESS TECHNIQUES, ONE BY ONE YOUR STRESS BUTTONS WILL BE DEFUSED. YOU ARE BECOMING A MORE RELAXED AND HEALTHIER YOU!

Some Final Tips

This book has taught you a repertoire of techniques for dealing with life's daily stresses. Some of the techniques will help you in specific situations; others will help you to control your general stress levels. We encourage you to review and redo all the Less Stress Lessons, to discover which techniques feel most comfortable and useful to you and to continue integrating these new skills into your everyday life.

In dealing with almost every daily stressful situation, other than emergencies which require immediate, fight-or-flight reactions, we've found two basic steps from our Lessons that can help you respond in a less stressful way. These are:

Step One: Use your favorite relaxation technique to lessen your physical and mental tension. You can use anything from a ten-second breathing awareness exercise to a full fifteen-minute session depending on the situation.

Step Two: When you feel a bit more relaxed, tune into your Mind Chatter. Notice if it is High Stress Mind Chatter based on High Stress Beliefs. If so, substitute Less Stress Mind Chatter and Less Stress Beliefs. You can easily do this step silently, in your mind.

After some practice you will be able to do these two steps in minutes, and the result usually will be a decrease in physical and mental tension. Taking the time to do these two simple steps will help you think creatively about how to deal with the stressful event. You will be able to make more skillful choices of action or behavior, which can lead you to less stress.

Here are three examples of how you can apply these two steps:

* * *

You're stuck in terrible traffic, and in ten minutes you'll be late for a crucial job interview. There's no phone booth in sight.

Step One: Choose a relaxation technique that you can do quickly and easily in your car. You could use any of the breathing techniques you have learned, or you could also try some progressive relaxation—tightening and relaxing tense muscle groups. You could do some gentle stretching when the traffic isn't moving at all. (Be sure to keep your eyes *open* at all times!) By bringing your attention to relaxation you can take your mind off the frustration of being stuck in traffic—which is out of your control—and use this time to nurture yourself instead.

Step Two: When you feel a little less tense, tune into your Mind Chatter. You might hear yourself saying:

"I'm such a screw-up. I should have left much earlier."

or "They'll never believe me when I tell them about the traffic."

Instead of focusing on this stress-producing monologue you can consciously change your statements to Less Stress Mind Chatter. For example, you could tell yourself:

"Worrying now won't get me there any faster and will make me more anxious when I arrive."

or "I can convince them that I'm an excellent candidate for this job even if I arrive late for the interview."

or "The interviewer has probably been stuck in traffic,

too. She will believe me and understand when I explain the situation."

or "If I don't get this job, it won't be the end of the world. I can find another one."

Learning to stay relaxed when you can't change your circumstances is a key to less stress.

* * *

The phone rings and it's your cousin announcing that he, his snobby wife, and their children just happen to be in the neighborhood and are planning to stop by for a visit in about an hour. You agree to the visit—you like your cousin—but your house is a mess. After hanging up you begin madly dashing around the house, trying to create some order out of the chaos.

STEP ONE: In this situation it is easy to take the time to do any relaxation technique you choose. You could try a few minutes of diaphragmatic breathing. Or you could sit down and repeat to yourself, "My breath is calm and regular," until you feel your breath becoming more calm.

STEP TWO: When you feel more relaxed, take a few minutes to examine your Mind Chatter and your Beliefs. You might notice yourself saying:

"I have to impress them or they'll tell the whole family I'm a slob."

or "I want them to like me, but I have to be better than I am to deserve their approval."

Don't focus on these stress-producing statements. Instead, substitute Less Stress Mind Chatter and Less Stress Beliefs. Try telling yourself:

"It's more important to feel relaxed than to have a neat-looking house."

or "I don't need to impress anyone else. I'm good enough just as I am."

or "It's okay to be sloppy if I choose to be."

or "It doesn't matter if my cousin's wife likes me or thinks I'm up to her standards. I like me."

or "I can clean the house in a relaxed way. Whatever gets done, gets done."

You can now make a balanced, reasonable decision about whether to clean your house. If you decide to clean up, try to relax as you do the work. Keep your awareness on whatever you are doing in each moment, rather than on what you must accomplish before the guests arrive.

* * *

You're at work and it's almost 4:30 P.M. You have two top-priority deadlines to meet today, and you have to pick up your child from the baby-sitter no later than 6:00 P.M. You find yourself going from one project to the other and getting very little accomplished. Everyone else has their own time pressures, so there's no way you can delegate any part of your work to someone else. Your boss is breathing down your neck . . . and you can feel the knots in your neck beginning to tighten, signaling the onset of another tension headache.

STEP ONE: Take a few minutes to go into your office or the restroom and use your favorite relaxation technique. You can use any exercise, but you might find it especially useful to try some image rehearsal. Visualize yourself accomplishing the tasks in an organized and efficient manner. Or, you can imagine yourself negotiating for extra time with the boss. When you return to your work, try using some of the breathing awareness techniques. Make sure you are breathing nice, deep, natural, diaphragmatic breaths, and send some relaxing breaths into the knots in your neck, softening and releasing the tension in that area. This can help you to concentrate and focus on your work, and it can give you the energy to do as much as possible. Remember: This is not a life-or-death situation and not worth the negative side effects of a full-blown fight-or-flight reaction.

STEP TWO: Take a few moments to examine your Mind Chatter and your Beliefs. You might notice that you are saying:

"I'm a failure."

or "I'll never get ahead if I don't finish these projects."

or "I should take a position with less responsibility."

Instead of focusing on these stress-producing statements, substitute some Less Stress Mind Chatter and Less Stress Beliefs. Try telling yourself:

"If I concentrate and work on one thing at a time, I will have a better chance to accomplish more."

or "If I don't finish these projects today, I can negotiate with my boss to finish them tonight at home or tomorrow. I will simply say that I wasn't able to do it. I won't be defensive."

or "I know I'm a good and honest worker. This is the best I can do."

or "It's okay to make mistakes. Even if I take a less responsible job, I'm still a good person."

* * *

These two steps will only take a few minutes, but they can greatly improve your ability to work efficiently.

As you begin to use these two steps in your own stressful situations, you may begin to see how the Less Stress Lessons can make your life less stressful on a daily basis.

Conclusion

"It takes twenty years to make an overnight success."
—Eddie Cantor

In the one month or more it has taken you to do all the Less Stress Lessons, you have probably seen many changes in the way you understand and relate to stress. You've learned to experience physiological and deep inner relaxation. You've discovered new ways of seeing and thinking about your life.

You also may have seen that you still need some help in order to change certain behavioral patterns. Old conditioning can be very powerful, and we often need outside help to uncover the deeper roots of our behavior and, ultimately, to uproot and replace these behaviors with new, more skillful ways of being in the world. Now that you've learned how to take time to nurture yourself on a daily basis, you may wish to put a high priority on taking more time for self-nourishment. You might want to continue working on your new Less Stress Goals with the help of classes, workshops, therapy, or by setting up an exercise and nutrition program under the guidance of a qualified professional. Or you might find that reading many of the books in our Suggested Reading list (p. 144) will help you to continue your progress. At the very least we recommend that you redo the Less Stress Lessons at least once, so they become an integral part of your daily life.

Although you have just finished the Less Stress Program, this is only the beginning of a less stressful life for you. There is no way to predict or completely control your external circumstances, but you have probably found some better ways to ride the inevitable waves with more balance and courage. As you continue your journey, we hope that you will allow the keys to stress management—*awareness, patience, self-acceptance, and acceptance of life's constant changes*—to be your companions for the rest of your life.

The authors would appreciate hearing from any readers who have questions or comments about LESS STRESS IN 30 DAYS. We'd like to hear how it helped you deal more effectively with stress, as well as any suggestions you may have about any aspect of this book. We will use your feedback and your anecdotes (with permission) in later editions of this book. Please send all correspondence to us in care of New American Library, 1633 Broadway, New York, New York 10019.

Suggested Reading

Stress

Benson, Herbert. *The Relaxation Response*. New York: William Morrow and Company. 1975. (pb.: New York: Avon. 1976). *A classic in the field.*

Davis, M., E. Eshelman, and M. McKay. *The Relaxation and Stress Reduction Workbook*. Richmond, CA: New Harbinger Publications, 1981. *A comprehensive workbook, detailing a variety of stress reduction techniques.*

Goleman, Daniel and Tara. *The Relaxed Body Book*. New York: Doubleday, 1986. *A variety of exercises to help you relax your body.*

Levinson, Harry. *Executive Stress*. New York: New American Library, 1975. *A discussion of living with stress within professional and managerial positions.*

Neurnberger, Phil. *Freedom from Stress: A Holistic Approach*. Honesdale, PA: Himalayan International Institute of Yoga Science and Philosophy, 1981. *A very thorough explanation of the psychological causes of stress.*

Ornish, Dean. *Stress, Diet and Your Heart*. New York: Holt, Rinehart and Winston, 1983. *An excellent and readable book on the relationship between heart disease and stress. Recipes for a low-fat diet are included.*

Pelletier, Kenneth. *Mind as Healer, Mind as Slayer: A Holistic Approach to Preventing Stress Disorders*. New York: Dell, 1976. *Applies current knowledge of stress to the medical problems many of us face.*

Selye, Hans. *The Stress of Life*. New York: McGraw-Hill, 1956. *The classic work on stress written by the primary authority. Parts of this book are highly technical but very well worth reading.*

———. *Stress without Distress*. Philadelphia: Lippincott, 1974. *A shorter, less technical book that discusses the difference between healthy stress and the type that destroys.*

Tubesing, Donald. *Kicking Your Stress Habits*. New York: Signet, 1981. *A workbook that helps you analyze your stress patterns.*

Health and Wellness

Ardell, Donald. *High Level Wellness*. New York: Bantam, 1977. *A clear guide to taking responsibility for your own health. A classic.*

Blanchard, Kenneth, Edington, D. W., and M. Blanchard. *The One Minute Manager Gets Fit*. New York: William Morrow & Co., Inc., 1986. *Four important fitness concepts help you make a lifetime commitment to well-being.*

Cousins, Norman. *Anatomy of an Illness from the Point of View of the Patient*. New York: Norton, 1979. *A well-known writer fights a usually fatal disease with laughter and attitudinal change. This book was the basis for a TV movie in 1984. Cousins also has a newer book on dealing with a heart attack, called* The Healing Heart. *Read these books even if you are completely healthy.*

Friedman, M., and R. H. Rosenman. *Type A Behavior and Your Heart*. New York: Knopf, 1974. *Well-respected, easy-to-read book by two cardiologists about the relationship between personality and heart disease.*

Gallwey, W. Timothy. *The Inner Game of Tennis*. New York: Bantam, 1974. *An easy-to-follow guide to the use of relaxation in the learning of a sport. An excellent book even if you have no interest in tennis or sports.*

Samuels, M., and H. Z. Bennett. *The Well Body Book*. New York: Random House/Bookworks, 1973. *Every household could benefit from this well-written self-help, self-discovery book. Teaches you to participate in improving your health.*

Simonton, O. Carl, and Stephanie Matthews-Simonton. *Getting Well Again*. Los Angeles: J. P. Tarcher, 1978. *The use of visualization and relaxation techniques in the treatment of disease, especially cancer, written by an oncologist and his ex-wife, a family therapist.*

Exercise and Nutrition

Anderson, Bob. *Stretching*. California: Shelter Publications, 1980. *An illustrated, easy to follow workbook of safe stretching exercises.*

Bender, Ruth. *Be Young and Flexible After 30, 40, 50, 60*. Avon, Connecticut: Ruben Publishing, 1976. *An illustrated guide to exercises based on yoga, suitable for beginners of all ages.*

Brody, Jane. *Jane Brody's Nutrition Book*. New York: W. W. Norton, 1981. *Down-to-earth advice.*

Christensen, A., and Rankin, C. *Easy Does It Yoga*. New York: Harper and Row, 1979. *A well-illustrated guidebook to gentle stretching exercises designed especially for beginners, for people with injuries or diseases, and for people over fifty. Many of the models used are in their seventies and older.*

Psychology and Meditation

Bach, George, and Peter Wyden. *The Intimate Enemy: How to Fight Fair in Love and Marriage*. New York: Avon, 1968. *For couples. How to recognize fighting styles, learn skillful ways to express anger and negotiate conflict.*

Dass, Ram. *Journey of Awakening: A Meditator's Guidebook*. New York: Bantam, 1978. *All of Ram Dass's books are worth careful reading.* Grist for the Mill *and* The Only Dance There Is *discuss stress from spiritual and psychological viewpoints.*

Dyer, Wayne. *Your Erroneous Zones*. New York: Avon, 1976. *How negative emotions, attitudes, and beliefs produce disease. A funny book.*

Ellis, A., and Harper, R. *A New Guide to Rational Living*. Los Angeles: Wilshire, 1975. *An explanation, with examples, of Rational–Emotive Psychology.*

Fields, Rick, Peggy Taylor, and Rick Ingrasci. *Chop Wood, Carry Water*. Los Angeles: Tarcher, 1985. *A practical guide to finding spiritual fulfillment in everyday life, with chapters on sex, family, work, money, healing, etc.*

Foundation for Inner Peace. *A Course in Miracles*. Tiburon, CA, 1976. *A daily guide for 365 days of lessons in love and forgiveness. Available from The Foundation for Inner Peace, P.O. Box 635, Tiburon, CA 94920.*

Frankl, Victor E. *Man's Search for Meaning*. New York: Pocket Books, 1963. *The author's understanding of meaning formed in the concentration camps of Germany during World War II.*

Goleman, Daniel. *Vital Lies, Simple Truths*. New York: Simon and Schuster, 1985. *The role of self-deception in our lives.*

James, Muriel, and Dorothy Jongeward. *Born to Win: Transactional Analysis with Gestalt Experiments*. Reading, MA: Addison-Wesley, 1973. *Uses experiential techniques to stimulate self-knowledge.*

Jampolsky, Gerald. *Love is Letting Go of Fear*. New York: Bantam, 1979. *An excellent daily lesson plan to help us live and love more peacefully.*

LeShan. L. *How to Meditate*. New York: Bantam, 1974. *An easy-to-follow overview of meditation techniques.*

Levine, Stephen. *A Gradual Awakening*. New York: Doubleday, 1979. *A very simple, but very powerful, description of meditation practice and the growth of wisdom and compassion.*

———. *Who Dies?* New York: Doubleday, 1982. *A book that*

explores our concepts and feelings about death. You should definitely read his most recent book, Meetings at the Edge, *especially if you have been dealing with the illness or death of a close person in your life.*

Peck, Scott. *The Road Less Traveled.* New York: Simon and Schuster, 1978. *Longtime best-seller on love, values, and spiritual growth.*

Rubin, Theodore. *The Angry Book.* New York: Macmillan, 1969. *Steps for dealing with anger constructively.*

Satir, Virginia. *Self-Esteem.* Millbrae, CA: Celestial Arts, 1975. *A clear, concise book on learning to respect and care for yourself.*

Walsh, R., and Vaughan Walsh, eds. *Accept This Gift: Selections From a Course in Miracles.* Los Angeles: J. P. Tarcher, 1983. *Helpful psychological and spiritual insights.*

Assertiveness

Blanchard, Kenneth, and S. Johnson. *The One Minute Manager.* New York: Berkley, 1983. *An excellent resource for business people. Best-seller.*

Bloom, L., K. Coburn, and J. Pearlman. *The New Assertive Woman.* New York: Dell, 1976. *Excellent self-help book.*

Dyer, Wayne. *Pulling Your Own Strings.* New York: Avon, 1978. *How not to be a victim.*

Smith, M. *When I Say No, I Feel Guilty.* New York: Bantam, 1975. *Learning to take better care of yourself.*

Visualization

Hendricks, G. *The Centering Books.* Englewood Cliffs, NJ: Prentice-Hall, 1975. *Two volumes for use by parents or teachers with children. Excellent exercises that teach relaxation, imagination, and communication skills.*

Masters, Robert, and Jean Houston. *Mind Games.* New York: Dell, 1973. *Exercises to expand your awareness.*

Samuels, Mike, and Nancy Samuels. *Seeing with the Mind's Eye.* New York: Random House, 1975. *A beautiful book that describes many visualization techniques.*

Time Management

Cooper, Joseph D. *How to Get More Done in Less Time,* rev. ed. Garden City, NY: Doubleday, 1971. *An extensive and detailed treatment.*

Drucker, Peter F. *The Effective Executive.* New York: Harper and Row, 1967. *Improving your effectiveness as a manager.*

Lakein, Alan. *How to Get Control of Your Time and Your Life.*

New York: McKay, 1973. *The best-known popular treatment of time management. Emphasizes individual responsibility.*
Scott, Dru. *How to Put More Time in Your Life*. New York: New American Library, 1980. *Effective self-help techniques.*

Sexuality and Sensuality

Barbach, Lonnie. *For Yourself: The Fulfillment of Female Sexuality*. New York: Signet, 1975. *Learning how to be orgasmic.*
Boston Women's Health Book Collective. *Our Bodies, Ourselves*, rev. ed. New York: Simon and Schuster, 1984. *Excellent best-seller on all aspects of health including sexuality.*
Castleman, Michael. *Sexual Solutions: An Informative Guide*. New York: Simon and Schuster, 1980. *Written especially for men, but an excellent resource for couples. Includes a national directory of sex therapists.*
Comfort, Alex. *The Joy of Sex*. New York: Fireside/Simon and Schuster, 1972. *The classic in this field.*
Downing, George. *The Massage Book*. New York: Random House/Bookworks, 1972. *An excellent instruction book that will teach you to give and receive a great massage.*
Heidenstan, David, ed. *Man's Body: An Owner's Manual*. New York: Paddington, 1976. *Self-help book for men.*
Rush, Anne Kent. *Getting Clear*. New York: Random House/Bookworks, 1973. *A comprehensive guide to varied personal growth techniques.*

Resources For Tapes (Relaxation, Music, Lectures)

For an excellent free catalog of relaxation music and environmental music, (i.e. ocean sounds), write to:

Vital Body
42 Orchard St.
P.O. Box 1067
Manhasset, NY 11030

We buy many of our music and guided relaxation tapes at an excellent local bookstore. They provide mail orders and will give advice on selection over the telephone.

Beyond Words Bookstore
150 Main St.
Northampton, MA 01060
(413) 586-6304

There are many sources for high-quality tapes on personal, spiritual, and professional growth, as well as guides to meditation, relaxation, and movement exercises (including lectures by such renowned experts as Carl Rogers, Leo Buscaglia, Timothy Gallwey, and Gerald Jampolsky). These sources also have tapes for children (music and stories). Write or call for free catalogs.

B.M.A. Audio Cassettes
200 Park Ave. So.
New York, NY 10003

Dharma Seed Tape Library
P.O. Box 1041
Belchertown, MA 01007

Hanuman Foundation Tape Library
Box 61498
Santa Cruz, CA 95061

Kripalu Shop
Box 793
Lenox, MA 01240
(excellent guided movement sessions on tape)

Omega Institute for Holistic Studies Tape Shop
Lake Drive
R.D. 2, Box 377
Rhinebeck, NY 12572

Soundworks
911 N. Fillmore St.
Arlington, VA 22201
(800) 422-0111 (9 A.M. to 9 P.M. EST)

Places to Go for Workshops

Write to the following for catalogs of the offerings of several well-known centers for education in health and wellness:

Esalen Institute
Big Sur, CA 93920

Hollyhock Farm
Box 127
Manson's Landing
Cortes Island, B.C.
Canada, V0P 1K0
(summer programs)

Insight Meditation Center
Pleasant St.
Barre, MA 01005

Interface
552 Main St.
Watertown, MA 02172

Kripalu Institute
Box 793
Lenox, MA 01240

Naropa Institute
Dept. NAF
2130 Arapahoe Ave.
Boulder, CO 80302

New York Open Center
83 Spring Street
New York, NY 10012

Northern Pines Wholistic Health Retreat
Box 279, Route 85
Raymond, ME 04071

Omega Institute for Holistic Studies
Lake Drive
R.D. 2, Box 377
Rhinebeck, NY 12572
(summer programs)

Rowe Conference Center
Kings Highway Rd.
Rowe, MA 01367
(summer programs for children and teenagers, as well as year-round programs for adults)

Sagamore Lodge and Conference Center
Sagamore Road
Raquette Lake, NY 13436

Spring Hill Farm
P.O. Box 124
Ashby, MA 01431-0124

Local health clubs, mental health centers, YMCAs, adult education classes, and medical clinics often offer workshops in stress management, exercise and nutrition, assertiveness, and communication skills.

Index